Naxalism and Maoism in India

Naxalism and Maoism in India

By

Prof S. Narayan

GYAN

ISBN: 978-81-212-1254-0

Price: ₹ 500

First Published, 2015

Published by

Gyan Publishing House
23, Main Ansari Road
Daryaganj, New Delhi-110002
Phones: 23282060, 23261060
Fax : 91-11-23285914
E-mail: books@gyanbooks.com

Laser Typesetting: Gyan Print, Delhi

Printed at: G. Print Process, Delhi

Cataloging in Publication Data—DK
Courtesy: D.K. Agencies (P) Ltd. <docinfo@dkagencies.com>

Narayan, S. *(Professor)* **, author.**
Naxalism and Maoism in India / by Prof S. Narayan.
pages cm
ISBN 9788121212540

1. Naxalite movement—India. 2. Communism—India. I. Title.

DDC 320.5320954 23

Contents

Preface

Most of the social scientists are of the opinion that Naxalism and Maoism is an outcome of lopsided development. I feel that the planning process has neglected the 'felt need' of the common man and policy and plans are based on 'assessed need', resulting into failure of the Government's programme and policy. Failure of programme and policy led to the birth of Naxalism and Maoism. The social and cultural milieu needs to be integrated with the policy and programme meant for the development of the people of India. Today, Naxalism and Maoism are considered to be the threat for internal security of the country. It deserves national as well as state-wise policy and programmes for the solution of this problem. There can't be single unilinear approach for the solution of this problem.

I have tried to explain in depth the issue of Naxalism and Maoism in the country with field data of Chhatisgarh and Jharkhand with passing reference of Odisha and Andhra Pradesh. The very subject of Naxalism and Maoism is a subject of disagreement. Different views are expressed by experts and analysts. Suggestions and observations are most welcome. Readers view will help me in bringing another volume on this issue.

I am thankful to Vikash Kumar for computer work and to Kalpaz for publishing it. I am in many ways thankful to my wife and children to allow me to work on this issue which generally social scientists do not like to work.

Prof S. Narayan

Section—A

In course of my anthropological and sociological study on causes, nature and dimensions of violence amongst tribals in various parts of India I had occasions to visit Bastar area of Chhatisgarh (which is now divided into separate revenue districts of Kanker, Bastar and Dantewada) and interact with anthropologists, sociologists and researchers working in the area, as well as the tribals and other people living in Bastar. What had struck me during these interactions was that while in most of the other tribal areas the tribal violence was in response to various developmental strategies of the government; in Bastar the government's initiative in this area was minimal. The only intervention of major significance was starting the iron ore project of NMDC in Bacheli and Kirandul areas. Though there were some tribal tensions caused by the imposition of Forest Conservation Act, the Bastar tribal was, by and large, a happy and satisfied person. There is a general belief held by many in Bastar that violence of the nature that is now witnessed in Bastar was brought by the naxalites from across the border of Andhra Pradesh. There is also a belief that the tribals of Bastar could be persuaded by the naxalites to take up arms and indulge in violence because the government had done very little for development of Bastar. There is also a view that the tardy pace of development in the area was the result of the belief that fast-paced development in the area would lead to 'traumatic encounters' of the tribal with a more complex, developed and, at times, exploitative group of people and that the tribal of Bastar should be very gradually integrated into the national mainstream of thinking, economic interactions and polity. The violence dimension in Bastar suddenly and steeply showed an upward trend with the starting of the Salwa Judum movement against the naxalites in Dantewada. Intra-tribal killings of this nature have not been seen in any tribal area of the country.

The tribal revolt was not only against Andhra naxalites operating in Bastar area but was also against their own tribesmen who supported the naxalites. The naxalites' retaliatory violence against the supporters of Salwa Judum was fast and chilling, leading to the Salwa Judum supporters running to police stations for protection which led to the setting up of Salwa Judum relief camps and pouring into Bastar area extra contingents of armed police. Things were still not very clear although press reports and articles gave a chronology of how Mahendra Karma, ex-CPI MLA of the area and now a Congress MLA, took over the leadership of the Salwa Judum movement; how this was not liked by a section within Congress who felt that Karma is acquiring an importance which he does not deserve; how the BJP Government led by Dr Raman Singh started backing Salwa Judum movement to compensate for his government's inability to use the police force effectively to encounter the naxalite menace in Bastar, etc. What was more surprising was a virtual war of words unleashed by the naxalites through various websites and study teams to highlight how the Salwa Judum and the State police can jointly unleashed violence and terror on hapless tribals of Bastar; how the state sponsored Salwa Judum movement has created violence and tensions between tribals living in Bastar, etc. On the other hand, the government of Chhatisgarh also responded through what seems 'sponsored articles' and pamphleteering to depict the naxalites as villains without any morals or ethics who are behind the violence created in Bastar area as well as against the Salwa Judum supporters who were forced to rebel against the atrocities committed by the naxalites and that the Government had no alternative but to protect the peace-loving Salwa Judum supporters against the violent naxalites. Between 17th and 22nd May 2006, members of an Independent Citizens Initiative consisting of Ram Chandra Guha (Historian), Haribansh (Editor, Prabhat Khabar, Ranchi), Farah Naqvi (Writer and Social Activist), E.A.S. Sarma (former Secretary, Government of India), Nandini Sunder (Professor of Sociology, Delhi University) and B.G. Verghese (former editor, *The Hindustan Times* and *The Indian Express*) visited Dantewada on a fact-finding mission. All the aforementioned persons are prolific writers and one has to only sample some of their articles to know their political leanings.

While three of the team members are constitutionalists with liberal socialist leanings, the other three are known to have pronounced leftist leanings, including one having strong pro-ultra left leaning. Though I do not see anything wrong in academicians having strong political leanings, I do feel that it does condition and contaminate empirical research. Further, a mere five-day field visit is too short a period to really understand the problem, especially a problem that is as complex as the one that has been developing in Bastar. As an anthropologist and a sociologist, the tribals of Bastar, their culture, their religion and their institutions have always attracted me. However, with the situation in Bastar becoming complex and violent because of the growth of naxalism in the area, Salwa Judum movement and the Government's response, I decided to constitute another team of anthropologists, sociologists, journalists and media persons, independent social thinkers and writers to visit Bastar area for a period of at least a month and visit various villages, haats, townships and talk to a large number of people–tribals, naxalites, settlers from other states, etc. All the team members have political leanings stretching from Gandhism to Marxism. However, all of us decided to put our personal leanings in abeyance and allow the facts to emanate from the discussions we would have with various persons in the area. We consciously decided not to talk to government servants because we felt that their responses would be similar to that of Chhatisgarh government. Similarly, the team decided not to talk to politicians because most of them would follow the known party lines. As concerned citizens, we do believe that no development in Bastar area is possible if peace does not prevail in the area. We also strongly believe that no development is possible unless the aspirations and fears of tribals of Bastar area are taken into consideration before planning developmental strategies in the area. We further believe that the tribals of Bastar will not be able to freely talk about their aspirations and fears unless they get the freedom to do so. A tribal cannot freely speak his mind under threat from the naxalites or the government. A situation has to be created in Bastar before development of the area as well as tribals living there can be earnestly undertaken. All the members of the team worked very hard not only by visiting various villages and haats but also by going through a wealth of anthropological and other literature on Bastar tribals, which included classical works of Verrier Elvin and Greigson as well as recent works done by contemporary anthropologists. This basic reading was required to develop an understanding of the ethos and culture of Bastar tribals as well as their behavioural and response patterns.

—Prof S. Narayan

Section—B

My romance with the tribals always inspire me to take up new challenges to work in tribal India. Though I had been to almost all tribal region and have worked on different dimensions of tribal India. Once while working on Rural Electrification in tribal India I had an occasion to visit Bero Block in mid-1970s. During this visit I got an opportunity to interact with Tana Bhagat. I was much impressed to observe their life style and Gandhian way of life. Since then I wanted to undertake research work on them. In 2010, I could fulfill my dream to work on Tana Bhagat. I personally went to field and stayed with them with the research team. My heart jumps out to see them and their economic condition. They are not sure to have two square meals throughout the year but even then they are leading the Gandhian way of life. The Naxalites come to their villages, beat them mercilessly but no reaction as they firmly believe in nonviolence and the result is that a few of Naxalites or Maoists changed their hearts and became Gandhian and permanently left visiting those villages in which Tana Bhagats live. They are wonderful living Gandhian, they deserve to be projected globally so that people may get inspired to see the living Gandhian. I am sure interaction with them may minimise Naxalism/Maoism though slowly but firmly and in the long perspective it can work as prescription to remove violence of any nature.

Prof S. Narayan

Maps

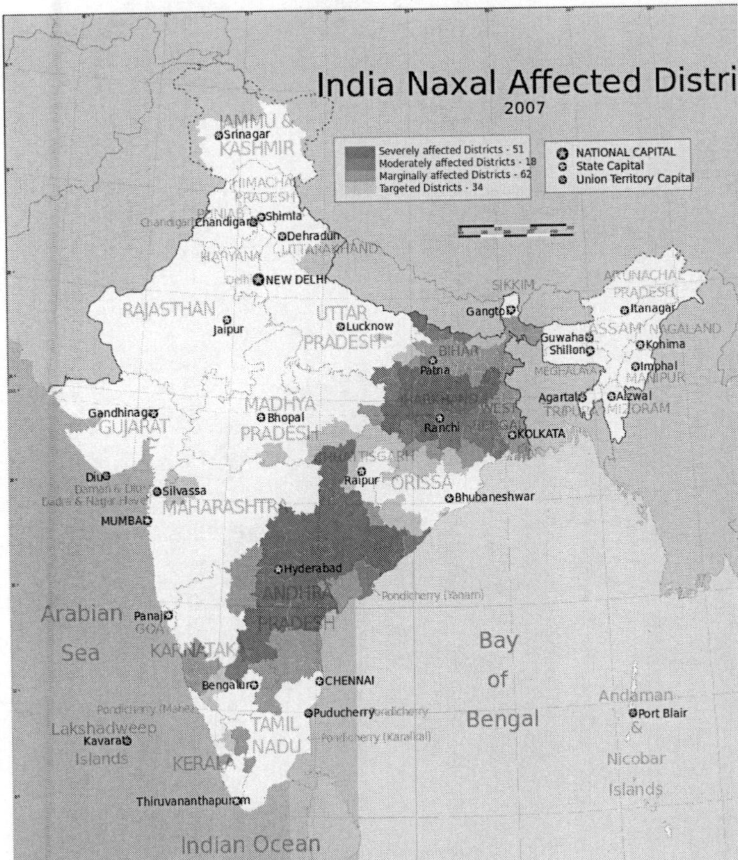

Naxal Affected Districts of India

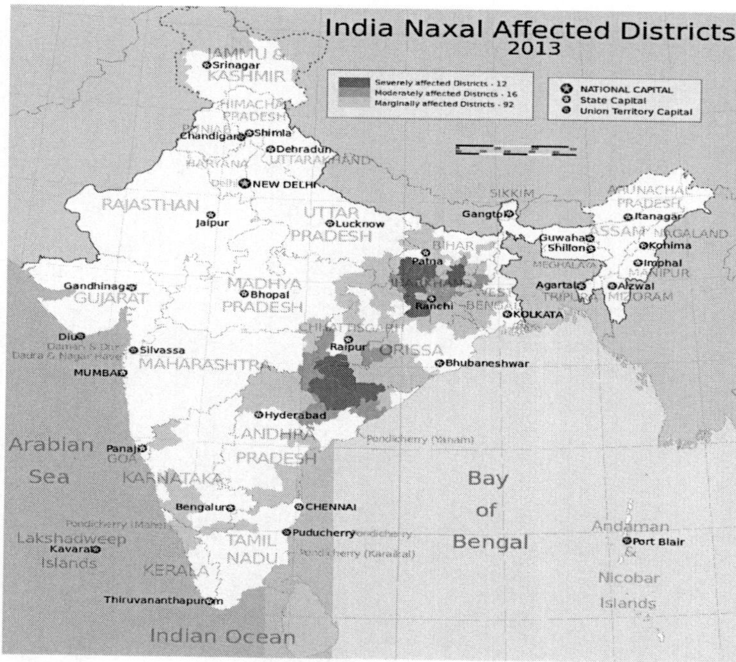

Naxal Affected Districts

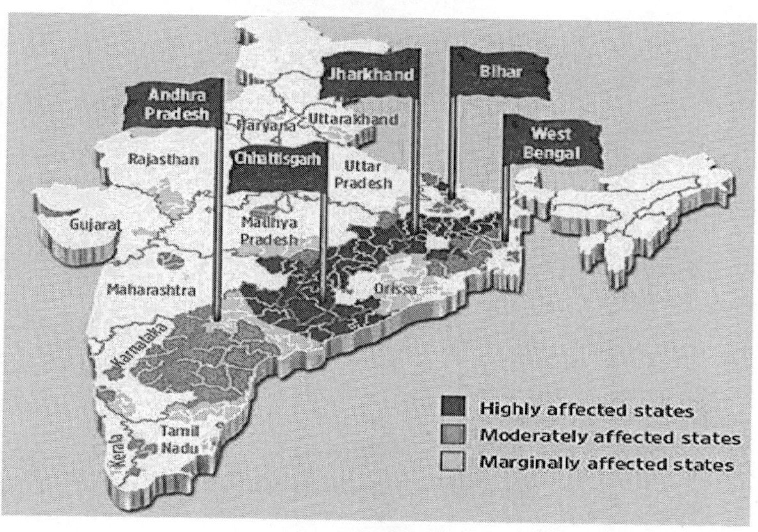

Naxal Affected States

Maps

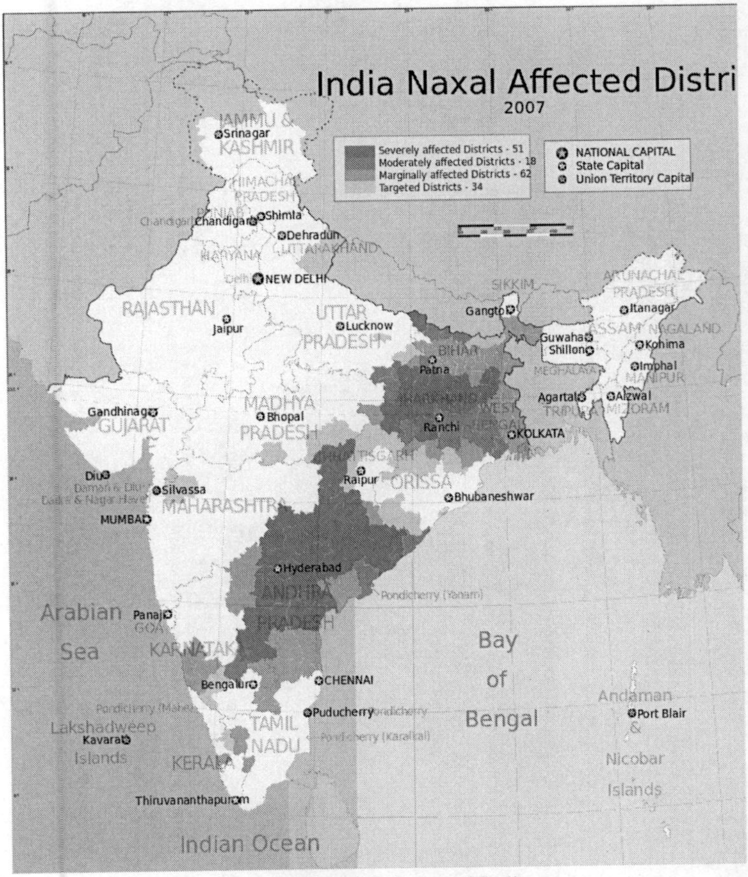

Naxal Affected Districts of India

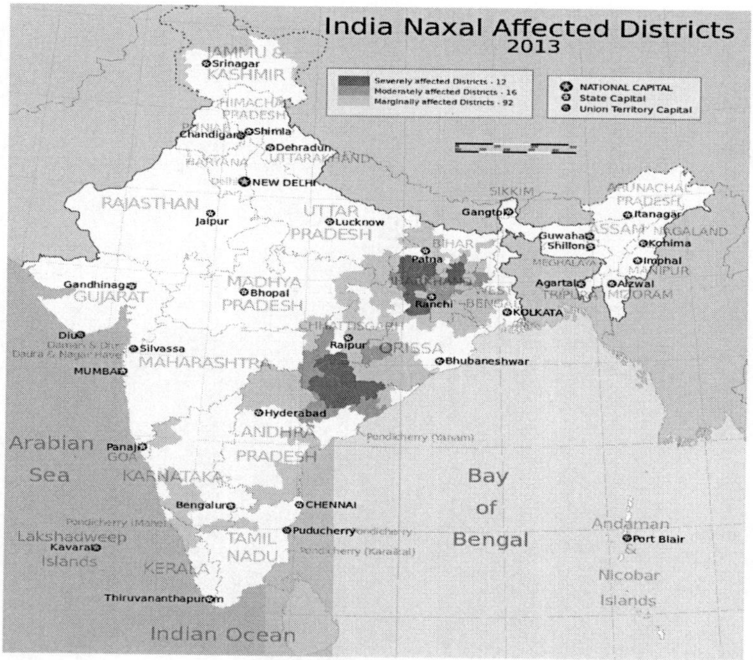

Naxal Affected Districts

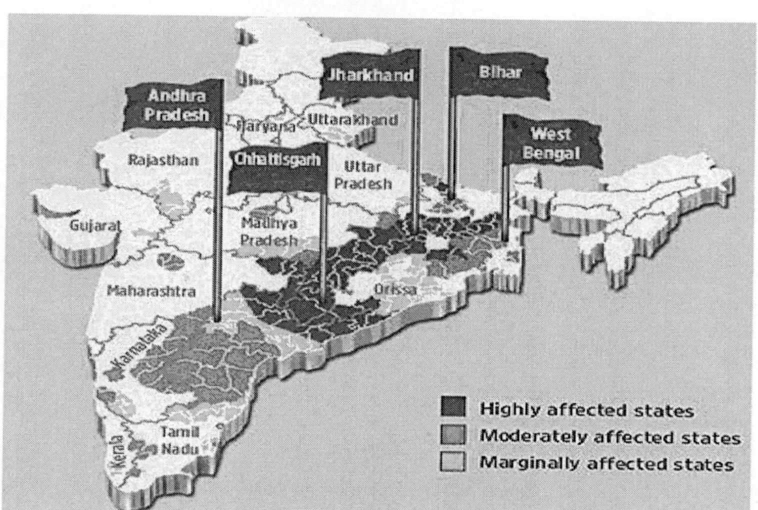

Naxal Affected States

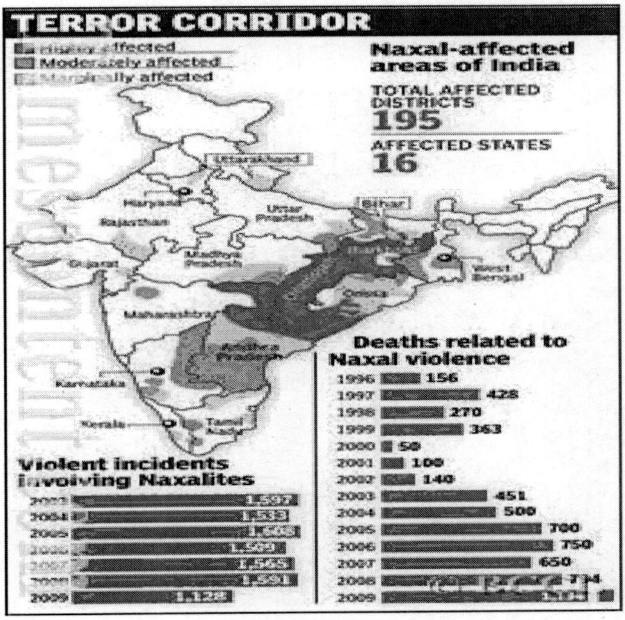

Terror Corrider

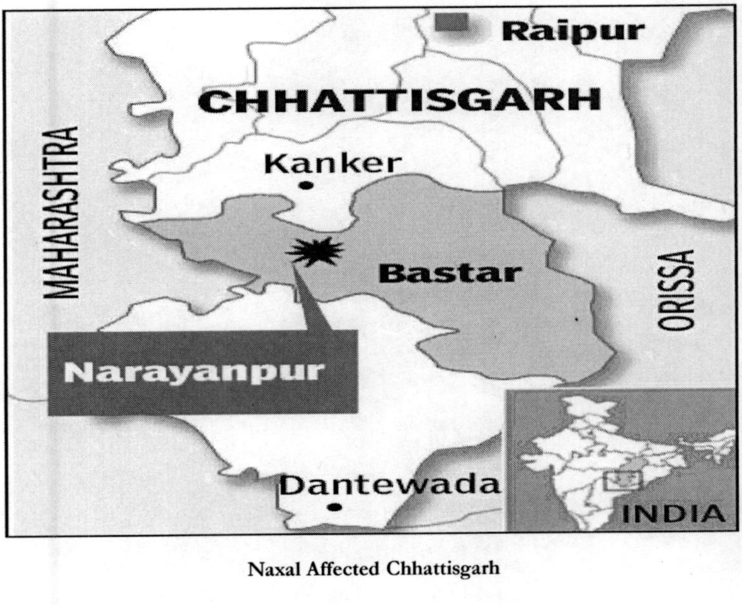

Naxal Affected Chhattisgarh

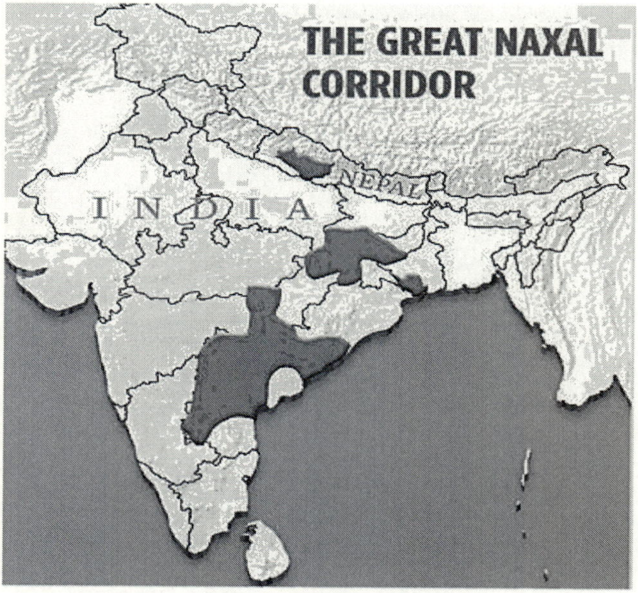

Naxal Corridor in India and Neighbouring Countries

Tana Bhagat in Lohandaga

Tana Bhagat in a Meeting

Ganga Tana Bhagat with Author

Introduction

Naxalism and Maoism is a social and cultural process of hardcore thinkers of the society, who wants to bring change through their hardcore activities. It has been observed, historically, that the changes took place when there is peace in the society. Social and economic development may take place when there is peace in the society. Revolution takes place through conflict and terrorism but not social and economic change.

Naxal, Naxalite and Naksalvadi are generic terms used to refer to various Communist guerrilla groups in India, mostly associated with the Communist Party of India (Maoist). The term 'Naxal' derives from the name of the village Naxalbari in West Bengal, where the movement had its origin. Naxalites are considered far-left tradical communists, supportive of Maoist political sentiment and ideology. Their origin can be traced to the split in 1967 of the Communist Party of India (Marxist), leading to the formation of the Communist Party of India (Marxist-Leninist). Initially the movement had its centre in West Bengal but gradually it spread into less developed areas of rural southern and eastern India, such as Chhatisgarh, Odisha, Bihar, Jharkhand and Andhra Pradesh through the activities of underground groups like the Communist Party of India (Maoist). For the past ten years, it has grown mostly from displaced tribals and natives who are fighting against exploitation from major Indian corporations and local officials whom they believe to be corrupt.

It is believed that in 2006 India's intelligence agency, the Research and Analysis Wing estimated that 20,000 armed-cadre Naxalites were operating in addition to 50,000 regular cadres and their growing influence prompted Indian Prime Minister Manmohan Singh to declare them to be the most serious internal threat to India's national security. Naxalites and other anti-government militants are often referred to as "ultras".

The present government led by Sri Narendra Modi, Prime Minister of India also believes that the Naxal and Maoist problem needs to be solved in the interest of the development of the people of India. Home Minister Sri Raj Nath Singh has also given several statements with regard to Naxalism and Maoism in India.

In February 2009, the Indian Central Government announced a new nationwide initiative, to be called the "Integrated Action Plan" (IAP) for broad, co-ordinated operations aimed at dealing with the Naxalite problem in all affected states (namely, Karnataka, Chhatisgarh, Odisha, Andhra Pradesh, Maharashtra, Jharkhand, Bihar, Uttar Pradesh and West Bengal). Importantly, this plan included funding for grass-roots economic development projects in Naxalite affected areas, as well as increased special police funding for better containment and reduction of Naxalite influence in these areas.

In 2009, Naxalites were active across approximately 180 districts in ten states of India. In August 2010, after the first full year of implementation of the national IAP programme, Karnataka was removed from the list of Naxalite affected states. In July 2011, the number of Naxalite affected areas was reduced to 83 districts in nine states (including 20 additional districts). In December 2011, the national government reported that the number of Naxalite-related deaths and injuries nationwide had gone down by nearly 50 per cent from 2010 levels. In 2014, the NDA government of Sri Narendra Modi has also claimed 25 per cent reduction in Naxal and Maoist movement.

History

The term Naxalites comes from Naxalbari, a small village in West Bengal, where a section of the Communist Party of India (Marxist) (CPI-M) led by Kanu Sanyal and Jangal Santhal initiated a violent uprising in 1967. On 18th May, 1967, the Siliguri Kishan Sabha, of which Jangal was the president, declared their support for the movement initiated by Kanu Sanyal and readiness to adopt armed struggle to redistribute land to the landless. The following week, a sharecropper near Naxalbari village was attacked by the landlord's men over a land dispute. On 24th May, when a police team arrived to arrest the peasant leaders, it was ambushed by a group of tribals led by Jangal Santhal, and a police inspector was killed in a hail of arrows. This event encouraged many Santhal tribals and other poor people to join the movement and to start attacking local landlords.

These conflicts go back to the failure of implementing the Fifth and Ninth Schedules of the Constitution of India. In theory these Schedules provide for a limited form of tribal autonomy with regard to exploiting natural resources on their lands, e.g., pharmaceutical and mining, and 'land ceiling laws', limiting the land to be possessed by landlords and distribution of excess land to landless farmers and labourers. The caste system is another important social aspect of these conflicts.

Mao Zedong provided ideological leadership for the Naxalbari movement, advocating that Indian peasants and lower class tribals overthrow the government and upper classes by force. A large number of urban elites were also attracted to the ideology, which spread through Charu Majumdar's writings, particularly the 'Historic Eight Documents' which formed the basis of Naxalite ideology.

At the time, the leaders of this revolt were members of the CPI(M), which joined a coalition government in West Bengal just a few months back. Leaders like land minister Hare Krishna Konar had been until recently "trumpeting revolutionary rhetoric, suggesting that militant confiscation of land was integral to the party's programme." However, now that they were in power, CPI(M) did not approve of the armed uprising, and all the leaders and a number of Calcutta sympathisers were expelled from the party.

Subsequently, in November 1967, this group, led by Sushital Ray Chowdhury, organised the All India Coordination Committee of Communist Revolutionaries (AICCCR). Violent uprisings were organised in several parts of the country. On April 22, 1969 (Lenin's birthday), the AICCCR gave birth to the Communist Party of India (Marxist Leninist) (CPI(ML)).

Practically, all Naxalite groups trace their origin to the CPI(ML). A separate offshoot from the beginning was the Maoist

Communist Centre, which evolved out of the Dakshin Desh group. The MCC later fused with the People's War Group to form the Communist Party of India (Maoist). A third offshoot was that of the Andhra revolutionary communists, mainly represented by the UCCRI(ML), following the mass line legacy of T. Nagi Reddy, which broke with the AICCCR at an early stage.

During the 1970s, the movement was fragmented into disputing factions. By 1980, it was estimated that around 30 Naxalite groups were active, with a combined membership of 30,000.

Violence in West Bengal

In Circa 1971 the Naxalites gained a strong presence among the radical sections of the student movement in Calcutta. Students left school to join the Naxalites. Majumdar, to entice more students into his organisation, declared that revolutionary warfare was to take place not only in the rural areas as before, but everywhere and spontaneously. Thus, Majumdar declared an "annihilation line", a dictum that Naxalites should assassinate individual "class enemies" (such as landlords, businessmen, university teachers, police officers, politicians of the right and left) and others.

Throughout Calcutta, schools were shut down. Naxalites took over Jadavpur University and used the machine shop facilities to make pipe guns to attack the police. Their headquarters became Presidency College, Kolkata. The Naxalites found supporters among some of the educated elite, and Delhi's prestigious St. Stephen's College, alma mater of many contemporary Indian leaders and thinkers, became a hotbed of Naxalite activities.

The chief minister, Siddhartha Shankar Ray of the Congress Party, instituted strong counter-measures against the Naxalites. The West Bengal police fought back to stop the Naxalites. The house of Somen Mitra, the Congress MLA of Sealdah, was allegedly turned into a torture chamber where Naxal students from Presidency College and CU were incarcerated illegally by police and the Congress cadres. CPI-M cadres were also involved in the "state terror". After suffering losses and facing the public rejection of Majumdar's "annihilation line", the Naxalites alleged human rights violations by the West Bengal police, who responded that the state was effectively fighting a civil war and that democratic peasantries had no place in a war, especially when the opponent did not fight within the norms of democracy and civility.

Large sections of the Naxal movement began to question Majumdar's leadership. In 1971 the CPI(ML) was split, as the Satyanarayan Singh revolted against Majumdar's leadership. In 1972 Majumdar was arrested by the police and died in Alipore Jail. His death accelerated the fragmentation of the movement.

2000 Onward

In a 2004 Indian Home Ministry estimate, their numbers were placed at that time at "9,300 hardcore underground cadre ... around 6,500 regular weapons beside a large number of unlicensed country-made arms". In 2006, according to Judith Vidal-Hall, "Figures (in that year) put the strength of the movement at 15,000, and claim the guerrillas control an estimated one fifth of India's forests, as well as being active in 160 of the country's 604 administrative districts." India's Research and Analysis Wing believed in 2006 that 20,000 Naxals were involved in the growing insurgency.

Today, some Naxalite groups have become legal organisations participating in parliamentary elections, such as the Communist Party of India (Marxist Leninist) Liberation, the Communist Party of India (Maoist) and the Communist Party of India (Marxist Leninist) Janashakti.

On April 6, 2010 Naxalites launched the most deadly assault in the history of the Naxalite movement by killing 76 security personnel. The attack was launched by upto 1,000 Naxalites in a well-planned attack, killing an estimated 76 CRPF policemen in two separate ambushes and wounding 50 others, in the remote jungles of Chhatisgarh's Dantewada district in Eastern/ Central India. On 17 May, Naxals blew up a bus on Dantewda–Sukhma road in Chhatisgarh, killing 15 policemen and 20 civilians. In the third Major attack by Naxals on 29 June, at least 26 personnel of the CRPF were killed in Narayanpur district of Chhatisgarh.

Despite the 2010 Chhatisgarh ambushes, the most recent central government campaign to contain and reduce the militant Naxalite presence appears to be having some success. States such as Madhya Pradesh have reported significant reduction in Naxalite activities as a result of their use of IAP funds for rural development within their states. The recent success in containing violence may be due to a combination of more state presence, but also due to the recent introduction of social security schemes, such as MGNREGA. In late 2011, Kishenji, the military leader of Communist Party of India (Maoist), was killed in an encounter with the joint operation forces, which was a huge blow to the Naxalite movement in eastern India.

In March 2012, Maoist rebels kidnapped two Italians in the eastern Indian state of Odisha, the first time Westerners were abducted there. Twelve CRPF personnel were killed on March 27, 2012 in a landmine blast triggered by suspected Naxalites in Gadchiroli district of Maharashtra.

Most recently on 25th May, 2013, Naxalites attacked a rally led by the Indian National Congress in Sukma village in Bastar Chhatisgarh, killing about 29 people. They killed senior party leader Mahendra Karma and Nand Kumar Patel and his son while in the attack another senior party leader Vidya Charan Shukla was severely wounded and later succumbed to his injuries on the 11th June.

On 11th March, 2014, Naxalites in Chhatisgarh ambushed a security team, killing 15 personnel, 11 of whom were from the CRPF. A civilian was also killed.

Cultural References

Satyajit Ray's 1971 film *Seemabaddha* was based on the life of an upper class family during the Naxalite Movement. *Erra* Cinema is a popular coinage in the south Indian language of Telugu referring to a collection of films many of which featured narratives in which a representation of Naxals and Maoists is attempted.

Khwaja Ahmad Abbas made a critically acclaimed film *The Naxalites* in 1980. It starred Mithun Chakraborty in the lead.

The British musical group Asian Dub foundation have a song called "Naxalite", which is featured on the sound track to the 1999 film Brokedown Palace.

The 2005 Bollywood movie *Tango Charlie* directed by Mani Shankar featuring Ajay Devgan had instances of the Naxalite movement and armed forces' counter operations.

A 2005 movie called *Hazaaron Khwaishein Aisi,* directed by Sudhir Mishra, was set against the backdrop of the Naxalite movement. In August 2008, Kabeer Kaushik's Chamku, starring Bobby Deol and Priyanka Chopra, explored the story of a boy who is brainwashed to take arms against the state.

In the novel *English August* by Upamanyu Chatterjee, there is reference to Naxal cadres whom the main protagonist, an IAS officer meets while visiting a tribal village in mid-1980s.

In the novel *The God of Small Things* by Arundhati Roy, there is a reference to a character joining the Naxalites.

In the novel *The White Tiger* by Aravind Adiga, the Naxals are mentioned often by the poor and the rich alike.

In the novel *A Fine Balance* by Rohinton Mistry, the character Omprakash makes and allusion to fighting "like the Naxalites".

In the 2012 novel "*The Truth*" by Michael Palin the protagonist Mabbutt is kidnapped by Naxalites whom are protecting his subject, Hamish Melville.

In the Indian novel *Red Jihad: Battle for South Asia* by Sami A. Khan, a splinter Naxalite faction (led by Comrade Agyaat) join hands with a Jihadi-cell (under Yasser Basheer) to destabilise a secular, democratic South Asia.

The 2013 novel *The Lowland* by Jhumpa Lahiri has one of the main characters involved in the Naxalite rebellion.

In 1974, Ramon Magsaysay Award winner Mahasweta Devi wrote *Hajar Churashir Maa* (Mother of 1084), giving an ideological and sympathetic support to the Naxalites. It was made to a film in 1998 naming *Hazaar Chaurasi Ki Maa*. It starred Jaya Bachchan as the mother of 1084, who was leader killed by the state.

The 2009, Malayalam movie *Thalappavu* portrays the story of Naxal Varghese, who was shot allegedly dead by the police during the 70s.

In the Kannada movie *Veerappa Nayaka*, Vishnuvardhan portrays a Gandhian whose son becomes a Naxalite.

The 2007, Kannada movie *Maathaad Maathaadu Mallige*, again portrays Vishnuvardhan as a Gandhian, who confronts a Naxalite

Sudeep and shows him that the ways adopted by Naxals will only lead to violence and will not achieve their objective.

Eka Nakshalwadya Cha Janma, (Marathi: The birth of a Naxal), a novel written by Vilas Balkrishna Manohar, a volunteer with the Lok Biradari Prakalp, is a fictional account of a Madia Gond Juru's unwilling journey of life his metamorphosis from an exploited nameless tribal to a Naxal.

In 2010, a Hindi drama movie *Red Alert: The War Within* was released that is based on the true story of a poor Andhra cook who gets caught in the gunfire between cops and Naxalites and is forced to work with the latter. In the 2011, Tamil political thriller film *Ko*, Naxalites are shown to rob a bank, overthrow the government and disrupt elections. At the end, it is shown that the naxalites were only used for political gains by the corrupt politicians.

Sindhooram, a National Award winning Telugu film released in 1997, portrays a young police officer becoming a naxalite under unavoidable circumstances. Directed by Krishna Vamsi, the movie was critically acclaimed for its direction and the performances of its lead actors.

Swayamsiddha is a 2010 Oriya film directed by Sudhanshu Mohan Sahu. The movie focuses on how and why people take to extremism, but overall it is a balanced movie and has messages for both the extremists and the government. The movie faced controversy as the main co-star of the film Siddhanta Mahapatra is an M.P. and belongs to the ruling party Biju Janata Dal of Odisha portrays himself as Maoist leader in the film, the opposition parties in the state went on strikes and demanded ban on release of the film.

Chakravyuh, a film by Prakash Jha, was released in 2012. It revolves around the theme of Naxalites, but received critical feedback for allegedly showing sympathy for Maoists.

Red Ant Dream, a documentary by Sanjay Kak, is based on the revolutionary Maoist movement in India. This documentary was under production for more than three years and released in 2013.

In his book named *Hello Bastar* writer Rahul Pandita has provided insights about the advent of Naxalism in Bastar district of Chhatisgarh and day to day life of Naxalites in the dense forests of this district.

Dantewada district, situated at the southern tip of Chhatisgarh, has borders with Maharashtra, Andhra Pradesh and Orissa, and was part of Bastar kingdom till 1947. After independence, it was merged with Kanker kingdom to form Bastar, the largest district (39,114 sq km) in the state of Madhya Pradesh. In 1998, Bastar was divided into three districts, Kanker, Bastar and Dantewada, and in 2001 all three districts became part of the newly formed state of Chhatisgarh. Recently, Bijapur has been carved out as a new police district in Dantewada. With a population of 7.91 lakh, Dantewada district has the lowest population density in the state at 40.8 persons per square kilometre (2001 census). Topographically, the region is composed of an undulating plateau, with hill ranges cut by a number of rivulets that flow into the Indrâvati River. These riverbeds provide the space for most rural settlements. Godavari and Mahanadi are two major rivers that arise from the Bastar uplands. The district is divided into four tehsils: Bhopal Patnam, Bijapur, Dantewada and Konta. The Salwa Judum and police operations originated in Bijapur tehsil, but have now spread to Konta. The people inhabiting the district are predominantly tribal and mostly Maria Gonds and Dorla accounting for 82 per cent of the rural population. Scheduled Castes account for about three per cent of 788 population and the rest are OBC communities like the Sundis, Kallars etc. A number of immigrants, mostly traders, but also lower level officials, school teachers, health workers etc., have settled in the small market towns like Bijapur, Sukma, Konta and Dantewada. The Bailadilla mines hardly employed any local adivasis, with the result that the mining town of Kirandul is a non-tribal enclave, with little connection to the surrounding countryside. This picture of a large number of fairly small tribal villages, and a few large villages, with on-tribal households is supported by the census data. Of the 1220 villages in the district, 455 are wholly tribal and another 458 are more than 90 per cent tribal, i.e., 75 per cent of the districts villages are almost completely tribal. Only 76 villages, or approximately six per cent of the larger villages serve as local markets and it is these that tend to have greater non-tribal populations. About 38 per cent of the rural area in the district is outside the village and part of forest land. The 2001 Census states these forests have

202 villages, of which about 90 are inhabited. What is pertinent is that these villages have no land rights and are at the mercy of the forest department. Dantewada has one National Park (Indrâvati) and two wildlife sanctuaries (Bhair-Amhgarh and Pamed). Other than these, the rest of the villages occupy 62 per cent of the district, but again 46 per cent of this is also designated as forest. Hence in total, about two-thirds of the district belongs to the Forest Department, at least on paper. Some of these forest areas may have been village lands earlier. For instance, in the areas under the Bhopalpatnam and Kutru zamindaris, feudal oppression during colonial times forced residents to flee their villages.

After 1947 and the abolition of Zamindari, these residents came back to find their lands notified as forests. The villagers are heavily dependent on both agriculture and forests. Of the total village land, barely 29 per cent land is cultivated, and as said earlier, nearly half is designated as forest and the rest is either uncultivable or is culturable waste. The average landholding per household (2001 Census) works out to 1.01 hectare, i.e., 2.5 acres. Irrigation being by and large absent (barely two per cent have some sort of irrigation), only a single crop is possible. The shifting of villages due to economic reasons is therefore common. In the 2001 Census, there are 30 such villages that have become uninhabited (this is in addition to 112 uninhabited forest villages). Some of these villages continue to practice shifting cultivation in forest areas, a practice that has been banned by the government, except in the Abujhmarh areas to the north of the Indravati. The land actually under cultivation may be significantly more than these figures suggest. Villagers have cleared significant areas designated as forest land within the village for cultivation. Most of the people own land, thus 84 per cent of the main workers in rural Dantewada and 55 per cent of the marginal workers are cultivators. Yet, the paucity of land and the low yields forces six per cent of the main workers and 39 per cent of the marginal workers to work as agricultural labour (in all, around 14 per cent of the total working population). Such employment is provided on the lands of those who own larger and/or more fertile plots. They work either as Naukar, i.e., free labour obtaining a seasonal wage, or as kabadi, i.e., attached labour with a larger landowner, getting food in lieu of wages. Such sale and purchase of labour is concentrated in some villages while being wholly absent in most others. Of the district's 1,220 villages, nearly 400 have no agricultural labourers and in all nearly 800 villages have less than 10 per cent, while 96 villages have more than 50 per cent agricultural labour. Labourers also migrate to neighbouring areas in Andhra Pradesh and Maharashtra for work. Given the rain-fed agriculture, the collection and sale of non-timber forest produce at weekly *haats* (markets) or to agents is an important source of local income, a fact that underlines the people is dependant on the forest, and their forced interaction with Forest Department officials and traders. At the village level, authority and respect is commanded by the Patel/pedda/mukhia (headman) and the priest. In some cases, the same person performed both functions. The next rung in the structure is the pargan manjh the head of a cluster of villages, a person of considerable clout. The headmen, in many instances, belong to households that are the oldest residents of the village, or those who initially set up village. The process of the shifting of populations led to later settlements within existing revenue villages, with the newer settlers obtaining lower amounts of land and less productive lands in comparison to the earlier settlers. Thus, while cultural practices ensure that economic differences are not visible in dress and size of dwelling, the older practice of collective labour has now become a means of garnering the labour of the less well-off by those better-off. Literacy levels are low in rural areas at 29 per cent for men and 14 per cent for women, with an overall rural literacy rate of 21 per cent. Yet this presents a partial picture. In Bijapur tehsil for instance, there are only 52 villages in which more than 25 per cent of the population is literate, and 35 villages have no literates at all. This is related to the availability and the quality of schools in the district; out of the 1220 villages, 214 do not have even a primary school and of these, for 107 villages the school is more than five kilometers away.

The presence of a school building in the village, moreover, does not ensure that teachers are available. In some cases, teachers use the excuse of the presence of Maoist organisations in the village to remain absent. In any case, with the ongoing Salwa Judum, schools have come under attack. Security forces have been using school buildings as temporary camps and Maoists have been blasting these buildings to prevent security forces from finding *pucca* shelters in the villages. The situation is distinctly worse regarding health facilities. Out of the 1220 villages, there is no medical facility in 1161 villages. A primary health centre exists only in 26 villages; a private registered medical practitioner in 17 villages, a government subsidised one in 12 and a community health worker in 122 villages. A comment on the inadequacy of the health infrastructure and the health and well-being of the people is provided through the studies conducted by Chhatisgarh PUCL in earlier years. As early as 1987, an investigation into repeated reports of blood dysentery in Bastar that claimed many lives each year revealed that people had very limited access to potable water. A more recent study during 2004 revealed that things had not really improved very much in the last 18 years. For the construcopment is to provide Rs 37.5 crore per annum for naxal-affected areas under the Prime Minister Grameen Swarojgar Yojana (PMGSY).

Indeed, what passes for development in official parlance has a security imprint. The physical infrastructure to be built includes—other than police stations—roads, bridges, etc. While roads, bridges and electrification will no doubt benefit ordinary people, it is evident that their needs are hardly what is behind the bringing in of the Border Roads Organisation for building roads in the region. An official Work Proposal from the collector office states that the real rationale of road building and widening is to flush the Maoists out from the jungles and make troop movement in the area easier (collector's Work Proposal). The BRO road from Jagdalpur to Dantewada, for instance, is not being built through the panchayats, and thus does not even provide local employment. To summarise, the adivasis and other local inhabitants of the region have little possibility of actual development and are acutely aware of their marginal and exploited status. For the overwhelming majority in the villages, agriculture is unviable since plots are small and there is no investment in irrigation, there are severe restrictions on the use of forests partly due to the creation of wildlife reserves, the prices of forest produce are deliberately kept low by traders and the government and the government machinery treats them with apathy and contempt. On the other hand, there is a small minority and mostly trading families, shopkeepers, members of the bureaucracy, lawyers and others living in the small towns, and some rich tribal leaders who have gained through politics or corruption involving illicit felling of trees Malik Makbuja Scam who want large development projects. In a situation where the state claims rights to the land and the people who live on that land are treated as peripheral to the national economy, a mass base of the Maoists challenging this *status quo* forms a threat to the state that plans for establishing heavy industry and profits in this region.

The first political mobilisation in the former Bastar district under the aegis of a political party took place in the mid-1970s, by the Communist Party of India (CPI). It created its organisation in the Bailadilla mines, around issues of control over mineral resources and work opportunities for locals. The struggle in the mines was brutally suppressed through state repression, including police firing on protesting workers during 1976-77 that resulted in the death of several workers and members of their families. The movement begun by the CPI spread through large areas of Bastar and brought the party electoral success in two of the three legislative assembly seats. The other issues taken up by them centred around the lack of amenities and access to forests.

The Government of India raises one or more India Reserve Battalions IRBs in each state. The concept of IRBs was mooted by the Ministry of Home Affairs in the background of increasing problems of law and order and emerging internal security scenario in the country, which put considerable pressure on the Central Police Forces. As of 2004-05, there were 85 IRBs in the country, each having 1,007 personnel. These battalions are trained by the CRPF and the BSF in fighting with modern weaponry. The responsibility for recruiting and maintaining these battalions rests with the state governments, but the central government bears the expenses towards raising and training its personnel. However, the central government has the power to deploy the IRBs anywhere on payment to the concerned state. (*Source*: Ministry of Home Affairs 2004-05.) Autonomous Council for the Bastar area to ensure a degree of independence in the formulation and implementation of development policy. Movements against the dominant development paradigm and rampant corruption in the administration continued throughout the 1980s and 1990s. Many of these were local in character. These included the movement against pine forestation to feed the Ballarshah Paper Industries, the movement of the women of Asna, Jagdalpur against forest enclosure and monoculture forestry, and the resistance of the tribals of Mawlibhata to a proposed steel plant on their land. In recent times, the most serious challenge to the dominant model of development has come from the CPI (Maoist) formations.

The Maoist Movement

The Telangana region of Andhra Pradesh, bordering Dantewada to the south, has a long history of peasant struggles dating back to the 1940s. By the 1970s, the struggles of the peasantry were led by a number of Marxist-Leninist parties, including CPI (ML) Peoples War (PWG), a precursor to the CPI (Maoist). Around 1980, PWG started an organisation in the area of present day Dantewada district, called the Dandakaranya Adivasi Kisan Mazdoor Sangha.

Malik Makbuja Scam: The Malik Makbuja right refers to the right of peasants to cut trees on their own land. A widespread scam in the 1990s led to the large scale illegal felling of trees in Bastar. It is a classic instance of how forest and timber resources in the region have been cornered by non-adivasi and adivasi elites. Ostensibly created to safeguard the interests of adivasis, the MP Protection of Scheduled Tribes (Interest in Trees) Act 1956-57 requires the supervision of the sale of felled trees by the Collector with the sale money being deposited in a joint account. However, agents soon took over the process by offering to help adivasis with the complex paperwork involved, only to cheat them. Timber merchants bought land in order to fell the trees on it. Since land alienation laws restrict the purchase of tribal land by non-tribals, timber merchants usually targeted the lands of poor non-tribal. However, rich tribal politicians such as Mahendra Karma were able to buy land from other tribals as well. Both revenue and forest staff facilitated this. Despite questions raised in the assembly by CPI MLA Manish Kunjam and others, and complaints of the Collector against his own superior for collusion in the Malik Makbuja scam, the MP government did nothing. Ekta Parishad and Samaj Parivartana Samudaya, two local organisations, took the matter to the Supreme Court [WP (Civil) No. 202 of 1995].

In 1997, the Court banned all felling in the then Bastar district of Madhya Pradesh. The Lokayukt held an independent enquiry and the matter was handed over to the CBI. A CBI FIR dated 8.12.1998 states: The facts contained in the writ petition, reports of Lok Ayukta and its connected papers, *prima facie* show that the above-named officials of Government of Madhya Pradesh and land owners namely, Mahendra Karma, Rajaram Todem, Suresh Chand Surana, Srinivasan Awasthi, Brij Mohan Gupta and others were party of criminal conspiracy during 1992–96 to cause wrongful gain to the land owners in the matter of felling trees. It is alleged that the accused public servants bestowed undue favours to the said land owners and others and illegally accorded permission to fell a large number of valuable timber trees on the basis of forged and fabricated documents and in utter disregard of the provisions of the MP Protection of Aboriginal Tribes (Interest in Trees) Rule 1957 and Madhya Pradesh Land Revenue Code 1959. According to a CBI letter dated 14.10.1999, FIRs had been filed against ten people for offences between 1992 and 1996 in 56 villages. However, no further action has been taken against Mahendra Karma or any of the other accused. Among the various explanations being provided today by the administration and sections of the media for the rise of the Salwa Judum, the ban on the sale of beedi leaf (tendu patta) by Maoists is often mentioned.

The year 2005 witnessed a strike call by the peasant organisation DAKMS that led to a boycott of tendu patta collection, an important source of income for tribal households. In the Dantewada region, 2005 was also a year of drought. Some discontentment over the boycott and the resultant loss in income among the adivasis is inevitable, but to say that it led to the Salwa Judum is absurd. Such theories negate the wider context for the ban, particularly of the long struggles fought by the adivasis and the Maoists to improve the rates of tendu patta, and the dubious role played by the state. For the large majority of Bastar's people, as also in the neighbouring tribal region of Gadchiroli in Maharashtra and Malkangiri in Orissa, incomes in cash result entirely from the sale of minor forest produce. Tendu patta, in particular, has a short season yet provides this income in the lean summer months and virtually every family engages in tendu patta collection. Tendu patta and bamboo also differ from other minor forest produce in that their collection and purchase is better organised, whether directly by the state or through contractors. Till the early 1980s, the tendu patta trade was wholly controlled by private contractors, and collection rates were extremely low, barely a couple of rupees for 100 bundles each of 100 leaves (i.e., for 10,000 leaves). By 1984, struggles taken up by adivasis and peasant organisations managed to raise the piece rates to Rs 17 per 100 bundles of 70 leaves each, i.e., Rs 24 for every 10,000 leaves. At varying times, state governments tried to abolish and replace private contractors. However these attempts failed as the governments prescribed rates much lower than those paid by contractors. In Maharashtra, the state government issued such an order in 1985, but was forced to withdraw it in 1989, following a boycott of tendu patta collection in the next three years. For Bastar, such a perverse order came in 1989; rates that had reached Rs 35 per 10,000 leaves were reduced by the government to a paltry Rs 25. Cooperative societies were formed to oversee its collection and purchase. This governmental policy resulted in a strike and led to a boycott of tendu patta collection for the next five years. From 1995, people in Bastar again resumed collection. They presented certain basic demands to the state government: A collection rate of Rs 100, establishment of a collection centre in each village, prompt payments, and the employment of local people as *munshi* and *watcher*. These demands were rejected. It led to varied protests ranging from mass petitions by villagers at forest range offices, to road blockades and destruction of forest produce depots. Protests persisted, forcing the MP government in 1999 to set up a committee to examine the fall in tendu patta collection. This committee recommended the re-introduction of the contractor system. During this decade from 1989 to 1999, the MP government had raised rates from Rs 25 to Rs 40 per 100 bundles. The reintroduction of the contractor system in Bastar witnessed a rise in rates from Rs 40 to Rs 80. Over the same period, rates by private contractors in Maharashtra had been hiked from Rs 60 to Rs 136. This was achieved through villager's tendu patta struggle committees negotiating with contractors. Police attempted to prevent negotiations and villagers were detained at many places. Contractors too were pressurised by the government not to agree.

The Ban on Sale of Tendu Patta continued with the demands. Despite this, rates in Maharashtra presently are Rs 180 but in neighbouring Bastar, the demand for a rate of Rs 100 has not been met, leading to a boycott of tendu patta collection. The above description makes it clear that the various state governments have played a most dubious role. They have viewed these struggles as increasing Maoists popularity and have tried to sabotage struggles. Despite this, increases in collection rates have occurred solely due to pressure from peasant organisations, which have used boycott calls as a form of struggle in bargaining with contractors and pressurising the government. Hence, notwithstanding some discontent to which it may have given rise, to say that the current ban led to mass support for the Salwa Judum is far from the truth. A more likely explanation of the relation between the boycott and the Salwa Judum is that the boycott further fostered the discontent of tendu patta traders and contractors, who had a grouse against the Maoists and who therefore readily made common cause with the government in the shape of the Salwa Judum. Porters and traders from small towns of Dantewada district, who have much to gain from industrialisation in the region, also play a prominent role in the Salwa Judum. However, what is important is that the state promptly exploited the situation. It is crucial never to forget that the Salwa Judum could not become what it has without the extent of state support it is getting. For instance, the District Collector told us that of the 150-200 Salwa Judum meetings that had been held till December 2005, he himself had attended 75 per cent. Other sources also make it evident that the state has played an active role in channelising and propagating the anti-Maoist opposition among sections of the population, thus fuelling the Salwa Judum as part of its all India anti-Naxal policy.

The Salwa Judum started on 1st June 2005 in Kutru, where people were upset with the Maoist is ban on collecting tendu leaves, the frequent closure of *haats* due to their bandh calls, and the alleged siphoning of development funds from the area. However, it also revealingly states that operation Salwa Judum was preceded by months of overt and covert operations by the police (from January 2005 onwards) in which the police tried in a subtle manner to convince people of the ills of Maoism. The video shots of Salwa Judum meetings clearly show the Chief Minister, the Collector and politicians like Mahendra Karma addressing these, and security personnel accompanying Salwa Judum processions. The video mentions the government concept of carpet security, by which military camps are stationed across the district, village defense samitis (organisations) created, and roadside settlements set up for those who can't return to their villages, for fear of Maoist attacks. Our fact-finding found that the carpet security plan was well in place. Also pointing to the administration is close and prompt links with the Salwa Judum is an audio CD released by the Maoists to the Chhatisgarh press in August 2005, in which the Superintendent of Police, Bijapur district, is heard stating that Rs two lakhs would be given to every village that joins the Salwa Judum. He is also announcing rewards for killing Maoists, and incentives for people with knowledge of weapons and landmines. It is instructive to learn that fostering local resistance is part of the government is all India policy to fight the Maoists. Annual reports of the Ministry of Home Affairs (MHA) for 2003-04 and 2004-05 refer specifically to the creation, raising, encouraging, promoting, etc., of local resistance groups and the need to harness the anti-naxal feeling among a section of the villagers to counter atrocities committed by naxalite outfits. Salwa Judum has become a part of conscious state policy. Without the state functionaries presence at meetings conducted by the Judum, and the state's role in conducting training for local Special Police Officers (SPOs) from among members of the Salwa Judum, fortifying police stations, building roads, maintaining camps, posting the Naga IRB in this region, etc., the Salwa Judum would not have become as powerful as it has. To understand the Salwa Judum, it is essential to look at the administration, financial and other kinds of support for it and the government's long-term anti-Naxal plans.

Mode of Operation of the Salwa Judum

This is what happened in Bangapal. On 3rd August we held a meeting in Munder village. Villagers from Munder ran away to the hills. The Naga Batallion went to the hills, caught them and brought them back, and made them join the Salwa Judum. Those who were unwilling to join were arrested. I don't know everything. I don't know how many people have been made to join and how many arrested, Lakshman Kashyap Local leader of Salwa Judum, in an interview said. No clearer account of what happens during a Salwa Judum operation is available. Those who don't join the Salwa Judum are forcibly brought in by the Salwa Judum members, the police and the Naga IRB. Both our fact-finding and an earlier fact-finding report (November 2005) by the Communist Party of India (CPI), point to a consistent pattern. First, Salwa Judum meetings are organised in villages that are known to support the Maoists. The audiences for these meetings are transported by buses hired or procured by the administration. Money for this comes from the central government. Often, various politicians address these meetings. Processions, called padyatras, go from the larger villages where camps are located and are accompanied by the security forces and sometimes, by the Collector or the SP. In the course of these meetings, the houses of sangham members or ordinary villagers are burnt and their cattle, pigs, poultry and other household goods looted. Since the houses in these villages are scattered, villagers are often unable to collectively resist these attacks.

However, some villages do resist attacks, aided by their own Sangham members and other Maoists. Sometimes people are killed, but no FIR is, ever registered for those killed by the security forces. Maoist killings are however, recorded and the family compensated in many cases. People from defeated villages are then forced to come and live in the camps, of which the administration itself claims to have set up seventeen. They are unable to continue with their agricultural activities and their normal existence, and are expected to go on Salwa Judum processions and meetings in other villages and be part of other attacking parties. Additionally, they are expected to keep an eye on people known to be associated with the Maoists. The daily lives of thousands of ordinary people in this area have been affected and their livelihoods hit by the Salwa Judum. In some places, such as Mankeli, in order to force the people to join, the Salwa Judum activists have prevented villagers from visiting weekly haats into purchase edible oil and salt. Individual families are sometimes split between the Salwa Judum and those who wish to remain in their villages or align with the Maoists. For instance, one of the men arrested from village Satwas, Barsu Sudru, has a younger brother who is with the Salwa Judum. The perma (priest) of Markapal is still in the village the team was not able to visit the village, but his wife has come to live in the Bhairamgarh camp. We came across instances where the Salwa Judum took away young people from their village and their families were unaware of their whereabouts. Since people who live in camps are forced to work as informers against members of their own and neighbouring villages, and participate in attacks against them, villages are becoming increasingly divided. Such divisions are of no small significance as either side is continuously engaged in violent attacks and killings. Sangham members who are arrested are kept in camps next to police stations or chowk is. According to the Collector, there are 1,500 surrendered sangham members in the camps. In February 2006, Mahendra Karma claimed that more than 3,000 sangham members had surrendered. The government has announced that it will give remobilisation grants to these surrendered Maoists. The men whom we met in camps openly stated that those who surrendered or were living in the camps had to keep informing the administration about the activities of the Maoists. Those who are reluctant to surrender remain in custody. Sukhmati of Taaki Lode village, north of the Indravati River was staying in Bhairamgarh camp because her husband had been locked up in the Bhairamgarh police station, located just behind the camp. This was when other men who lived in the camp were undergoing SPO training. The SHO of the Bhairamgarh police station, however, denied that there were any people locked up in the police station. Attacks by Salwa Judum unlike the Jan Jagrans of 1990 and 1998, when some mukhiyas were mobilised against the Maoists, now the attacks by the Salwa Judum on villages are being carried out with the assistance of the CRPF and the Naga IRB, accompanied by a small contingent of civilians. The Naga IRB, feared by the locals, is in fact known to prefer to conduct their raids by themselves. While we do not have any independent confirmation of this, there are serious allegations of rapes by security forces and Salwa Judum activists. Maoists have listed 31 cases of rape, of which six women were also murdered since the Salwa Judum began in June 2005. There also are reports that children and old people are being beaten. Villages are forcibly cleared of people and their cattle. In most villages that had been attacked, we found that entire villages were completely empty, except for the occasional old person and women in some cases. We also chanced upon villages where people had finally decided to surrender following repeated attacks by the Salwa Judum and the security forces. The following are accounts of some attacks on villages by the Salwa Judum.

Kotarapal Village

Kotarapal is a large village divided into Joona Kotarapal and Navin Kotarapal, which was a stronghold of the Maoists. Kotarapal was attacked four times by the Salwa Judum. The first was on 18th June 2005, following a Salwa Judum meeting at Matwada in which about 3,000 people participated. The meeting was addressed, among others, by Mahendra Karma Majhi, mukhiya Korsa Sukulu and Lekam Jilaram. People from villages close to the Indrâvati such as Sattuva, Bail and Dharma also participated. From the meeting, about a thousand people marched to Kotarapal village, a few kilometers away. Forewarned villagers had already sent the aged and the children out of the village; young men and women stayed back. When the Salwa Judum procession neared the village, it was attacked by the villagers and sangham members. In the melee that ensued, two people died. Sangham members detained 12 people, of whom 11 were later released. Bhuvneshwar Thakur of Jangla remained in their custody and he was killed on 26th June. Following the 18th June incident, a Salwa Judum meeting took place in Bijapur, called by Mahendra Karma, Prabhari Mantra Kedar Kashyap and Rajendra Pambhoi, MLA.

It was here that the Jan Jagran Abhiyan became Salwa Judum. On 1st July, Kotarapal was attacked, for the second time, by a combined force of the District Armed Force and the CRPF, which was led by the Inspector-General, Bastar region, the S.P. Bijapur, as well as Mahendra Karma. Since most of the villagers and sangham members had escaped to the jungle, the attackers looted and burnt their houses and killed their cattle and livestock. Two elderly peasants, Uikay Sannu and Vanjam Mangu, were killed and an old woman was fatally injured. The third attack took place on 11th August, in which Lekam Budhram (35) and Aatam Bodhi (30), both sangham members, were killed by Naga IRB soldiers. It appears that in this attack, as well as a fourth attack that followed on 12th September, Naga IRB soldiers took a large number of people to Matwada camp. According to the CPI fact-finding report, 48 youths who were allegedly sangham members were picked up from Kotarapal and made to surrender before Mahendra Karma on 13th October. Since then they have been detained in Bhairamgarh police station. According to some people from the village, whose families had refused to live in the camps, their mukhiya had been pressurising them to leave the village. Many people had already run away into the forests. The last two families from this village were attacked by the Naga IRB and the men taken away to nearby Jangla and tortured. The village now lies completely empty.

Munder Village

Munder village, another known Maoist stronghold, was almost entirely empty when we reached there. Road construction activity, which was on in full swing stopped about half a kilometre before Munder. In the village, we met one very old man who told us that everyone was out working on their fields. We found, strangely, that field after field was being harvested only by women. One woman told us that all men of working age from the village had been taken away by the Salwa Judum to Bangapal, which has a large SPO training camp, and had not returned home. Munder is eight kilometres from Pharasapal, Mahendra Karma's village. Munder village had been attacked five times. Munder was first looted on 22nd July. Pigs, goats and chicken were slaughtered and made a feast of and ten houses were burnt. There were no casualties because the villagers, many of whom are sangham members, were expecting an attack and had escaped to the nearby forest. Three days later, the village was again attacked. Three more attacks took place. In the first of these, on 28th August, Boggam Sannu (18 years) was killed. Then a meeting was called on 3rd September in Munder by the Salwa Judum. Once again the villagers escaped to the forest. According to Lakshman Kashyap, who was the local organiser of this attack, 10 girls and 11 boys escaped to the forest. This time, the Naga soldiers entered the forest, killed Kadli Kummal (a DAKMS member) and captured the rest, who were asked to join the Salwa Judum. Twelve people who refused were detained without being charged. On 10th September, in yet another attack, Kadli Kamlu (DAKMS member) was killed by Naga soldiers while they were on a patrol in the now-deserted village.

Mankeli Village

Mankeli is a large forest village, with several smaller hamlets off the road between Bijapur and Gangaloor. This village too has been repeatedly attacked. Out of approximately 112 houses in six hamlets, about 60 houses have been burnt by the Salwa Judum and several have been looted. The Murias of this village originally came from the Pinkonda area. Of all these households, only about 25 households had pattas given by the forest department. The rest cultivated encroached land. The Maoists redistributed land within the village for instance, five acres of one man is holding of 25 acres was taken for collective cultivation. The seeds from this farm were given to those who did not have any seeds for cultivation the following year. The Forest Department officials have not visited this area for two years. People here, like in many other places, complained about the ban on tendu leaves. In fact, they said they were warned that their hands would be cut off if they sold tendu leaves, but all in all, they came across as being neither with the Maoists, nor with the Salwa Judum. The first time the Salwa Judum came, on 15th September, the CRPF set fire to people is homes, including their pigsties. The Salwa Judum took away people is goats, pigs, poultry, and the mahua, tora and grain they had stored. They set 21 fires to the anganwadi building after looting the mahua, imli and other things that had been stored in it. They also killed 20-year old Modiyam Bhadru. The villagers buried his body and after this incident, no one wanted to join the Salwa Judum. Expectedly, the village was attacked again. This time, on 25th September, the Naga IRB soldiers came on their own and killed Korsa Suklu and Punem Kanda, both sangham members. The Naga forces also took away some 5-6 boys and one girl, who were forced to work as informers. The village headman was also taken away. The third time, on 3rd October, the Naga soldiers came with two of the boys they had taken away earlier, who identified two sangham members Kosa Aitu and Emla Kova. They were killed while working in their fields. The villagers were also told by the Salwa Judum, in turn, that since they gave shelter to the Maoists, they would not be allowed to purchase anything from the haats (markets). As a result, they could no longer buy even basic necessities like salt from Bijapur. Villagers also said that all the sangham members from Naya para (hamlet) had been captured while those in other paras of the village were in hiding. In Tong para, everyone, not just sangham members had fled. The Maoists broke down a school in this village in which Naga soldiers had spent a night. The villagers said that the Maoists had warned the sangham members that if they joined the Salwa Judum, they would be killed. The villagers had been sent a letter to join the Salwa Judum in September, and had already displayed some readiness to join the Salwa Judum by attending Salwa Judum meetings at Dhanar (1st October) and Korrepal village (4th October). These two villages had been spared because they had indicated a readiness to join in. When we met the villagers, three attacks by the Salwa Judum on the village had already taken place. They were extremely tense and were deliberating on whether and how to surrender to the police in Bijapur. Three paras hamlets had resolved to do this and thought that the others would join them. They were hoping that once they had officially surrendered they would be allowed to live normally. Even as we were in Mankeli, we heard gunshots, whose source we had no way of confirming. In front of us, three terrified men ran for their lives. What happened in Mankeli illustrates the manner in which villages with a Maoist mass base are, through coercive means, being annexed to the Salwa Judum campaign. A news report quotes a Dantewada DSP as saying, Rebels have been fast losing base in their stronghold in Dantewada district. Around 35 senior sangham members surrendered at a function in Mankeli village, 412 km south from state capital. Over 5,000 local people attended the function from 22 villages, completely hiding the brutal process by which this several such accounts such as Mankeli or Munder could be given, but we were unable to visit many villages because of the difficulty we faced in travelling freely in this region. Much of the information we have may be incomplete, simply because the administration keeps no account of the people killed or displaced by the security forces and the Salwa Judum. Nevertheless, we met people from different villages in camps who spoke about their displacement. For instance, in Bhairamgarh camp, we were told by the people of Halur village that they had been brought there by the Naga soldiers.

Maoist documents claim that many attacks of the Salwa Judum and the security forces have gone unrecorded. For instance, village Ariyal, a forest village which is a Maoist stronghold, where tensions had been brewing for long, was attacked on 2nd September. The mukhiya of Ariyal, Dorru Mangu, who had joined the Salwa Judum, led the attack in which ten sangham members, including a 12-year-old BAL sangham member were detained, made to stand in a row and shot dead. Amongst those who were killed, were relatives of the mukhiya himself (Prabhat, July-December 2005). A CPI fact-finding team had visited several villages, where they were told of the Salwa Judum looting, burning and killing. In village 22 Mundbedi, the CRPF had come accompanied by 50 Salwa Judum members. They took 40 kg rice from the house of Nandu, along with chickens, pigs, goat and whatever they could lay their hands on. The Salwa Judum burnt four of Kavad village 36 houses, and cooked within the village some of the things they looted 20 kg of rice, 20 chickens and one pig. The villagers hid in the forests. While leaving, the Salwa Judum burnt two quintals of kosra and 40 kg of rice. After emerging from Kavad village, the Salwa Judum attacked villages Pidiya and Andri. Thirty houses were burnt in village Pidiya, and Santu, son of Aitu, was shot dead by the CRPF. In village

Burji, the Salwa Judum forces came on 30th September and killed and ate six pigs and six chickens. They also took away 10 goats, 30 vessels mahua, and grain. Lemon and sulphi trees were cut and one cycle was broken. People from 60-70 houses ran away and the Salwa Judum looted Rs 10,000 from their houses. In village Mallur, a thousand-strong Salwa Judum procession came in October along with the CRPF. They beat up 17 youths badly and took them away, forcing them to join the Salwa Judum. Mallur, Palnar and Tamodi villages also suffered burning and looting. In Palnar, 30 people were forcibly taken away, of whom Sukhram, son of Godi, was killed. In the first week of August, in Manjhi-mendari village, a combined force of Salwa Judum and the police burnt all the houses as well as pigsties and chicken coops. All the pigs, goats and chickens were killed and eaten. The village was empty because when the attack began, the villagers ran away to the forests to escape the attack but didn't have time to take all their belongings.

Our team also met some villagers from these villages such as Burji, Pusnar, Palnar and Mallur in Gangaloor camp. Half the villages had come to live in camps while the other half was hiding in the jungles. Once in the camp, they are unable to do other work or return to cultivate their fields. They were also expected to turn up for Salwa Judum processions whenever they were called in other words, they were captive. CPI (Maoist) violence, the Salwa Judum has led to an increasing spiral of violence, in which both sides are now fighting an almost full-fledged war. This is in contrast to two people who are listed as killed in 2004, according to official documents.

During our fact-finding, we heard that in some cases, the Maoists had killed people simply for attending Salwa Judum meetings. One man from Palnar told us at Gangaloor camp that after a Salwa Judum meeting on 24th August in Gangaloor, the Maoists called a meeting in Palnar the next day and told people not to join the Salwa Judum, and noted the names of ten people, including him, who were taking others to join the Salwa Judum. He explained to the Maoists that he had taken people to avoid having the village burnt down. He was, however, threatened by people present from Saonar village for joining the Salwa Judum and as a result, had left the village out of fear. On 4th September, some Maoists came to Palnar and told people they had to leave their houses and camp in the hills to avoid attacks by the Salwa Judum. At 8 pm that night of 4th September, the sarpanch, the village patel and 7 SC boys were asked about their relationship with the Gangaloor Majhi and told that if they joined the Salwa Judum, they would not be allowed to come back and live in the village. The sarpanch, patel and two others were killed, while the remaining SC boys escaped to Gangaloor. Later, some of the people from Palnar who had camped in the hills came to Gangaloor. Of the 350 households in Palnar, about 50 went to Gangloor. They had left the Maoist camp on the pretext that they wanted to come back to the village to restock grain. Following this, their houses were raided and the school and hospital in Palnar destroyed by the Maoists. In Gongla, the 70-year old former sarpanch Gaita Budu took people from the village to a Salwa Judum meeting in Gangaloor on 21st September. The following night, Maoists came to his house and killed him. After this incident, the whole village went to Gangaloor. In Kotarapal village on 18th June, Bhuvneshwar Thakur of Jangla was first detained for being a Salwa Judum organiser and then killed by sangham members while he was already in their custody. We talked to people in Bhairamgarh camp, where there were about 2,000 people from around 25 villages. Some ordinary people who attended Salwa Judum meetings from curiosity or a desire to avoid having their villages attacked by Salwa Judum have also come into camps either out of fear of Maoists or specifically after being threatened by them. Individual families and villages are sometimes split between those joining the Salwa Judum and those who wish to remain in their villages or align with the Maoists.

For instance, while half the residents of Markapal village chose to stay on in the village, the other half had fled to the camp after sangham members threatened the men for attending a Salwa Judum meeting in Bhairamgarh. Those who had come to the camp had sold their mahua and left with whatever they had. Several people in Bhairamgarh camp and elsewhere told us of instances of threats and beatings when people chose not to ally with the Maoists. Pramod Kumar and Lakmibai from Maramatta village told us that the Maoists took away 30 quintals of their last crop along with Rs 15, 000. He also said that his entire village was threatened. Those who did not become sangham members or those who were sympathetic to the government policies were driven away. Villagers from Dharma village said they had heard that the Maoists would beat those who had come to camps, and were therefore scared of returning. The Maoists have since put out notices asking people in the camps to come back to their villages, assuring them that they will not be harmed besides fear of Maoist violence, some issues of coercion came up during our interviews. Some people from Gongla village complained that they were forced to give contributions to the Maoists in the form of one day tendu leaf collection and one day pruning wages, as well as rice contributions. Phulmati, whom we met in Jagdalpur Hospital, told us that she was forcibly taken away by Maoists to harvest grain elsewhere and her aged father who protested was beaten. People from Gongla said that no panchayat work was allowed in their area. The educated youth are unhappy with the Maoist opposition to government programmes. They want government programmes to be implemented as these are a source of employment. Not being able to participate in elections is also an issue for some people. There has been an intensification of the conflict by both sides in recent weeks. CPI (Maoist) squads have begun attacking and killing security forces stationed in Dantewada and elements that they perceive are in alliance with these forces. On 28th February, at least 26 persons were killed when Maoists used a landmine to blow up a truck near Konta, which was carrying people returning from a Salwa Judum meeting. In yet another landmine blast, 14 people were killed in Kanker district on 24th March, 2006 when Maoists attacked a jeep in which a group of tribal and local tradesmen were returning home from the local market. The Maoists targeted the private vehicle, mistaking it to be a police jeep. In the second incident the Maoists have apologised for the landmine blasts. The actual scale of Maoist violence tends to be exaggerated by the administration, helped by an ideologically bent and largely pliant media, to suggest the illegitimacy of the movement. A point repeated to us by everyone, including many Salwa Judum activists, was that the Maoist movement had a mass base among the poor for whom some very real victories have been won, especially against a corrupt officialdom.

It is, however, a fact that the escalation in violence has had certain unfortunate fall outs. In an area where medical and health facilities are already lacking, schools and hospitals are either rendered dysfunctional by their use as bases by the security forces, or are consequently destroyed by the Maoists. In the prevailing warlike situation the Maoists have used coercion and fear for purposes of intimidation, and shown a general intolerance of dissent. More disturbingly, the escalation in violence has resulted in a number of killings by the Maoists when the victims were in their custody and hence isolated and unarmed. The maintenance of democratic practices by people is movements are particularly important in furthering a progressively democratic society.

Displacement and Life in Camps the government has set up several camps in Dantewada for all those villagers who have had to vacate their homes, as a consequence of the Salwa Judum campaign. We found that these camps house five groups of people: those sarpanches, their families and allies who have a stake in working with the administration and who had decided to live in the camps because of Maoist threats; ordinary villagers who have been forced by the Salwa Judum to leave their villages and live in the camps; those who had fled their homes because of real incidents of or rumours about Maoist retaliatory violence; the SPOs and in some cases, their families; and lastly, surrendered sangham members and their families. All these camps have been set up near police stations. According to the Collector, Dantewada, there are 17 such camps, with approximately 15,000 people living in them in Bhairamgarh and Bijapur tehsils alone. In one camp in Bhairamgarh alone that we visited, there were 2,000 people from around 25 villages in the camp. Some of these consisted of entire villages such as Belnar, Bangoli, Sattuwa, while in other cases a few families from a village had come in. It is difficult to overstate the extent to which the daily lives of thousands of people have been turned upside down and their livelihoods destroyed due to the ongoing evacuation of villages. In many cases people were made to leave their villages soon after sowing and crops now lie rotting and uncut in the fields.

People living in camps that were relatively close to their villages trekked all the way every day to work on their fields.

Those who are under SPO training, however, spend their days being trained in the camp. They had been promised a monthly allowance of Rs 1,500. When people already are at the margins of poverty and then have their livelihoods hit, this becomes a despicable way the government is inducing people to take up arms in its offensive against the Maoists. Many others have started working on earth-works under the Food for Work programme of the central government. According to women from Markapal village we spoke to, the men got Rs 50 for doing coolie work; other reports suggest that people are getting Rs 55 to 60 a day for Block level or PWD work and Rs 60 for forest work. The roads that locals are working lead to police stations off the highway. Locals are not employed in the construction of the national highway NH 16, as the work was given to the Border Roads Organisation (BRO), which prefers to bring in workers from outside. Most people the team met said that they were surviving on whatever they brought with them initially or on meagre government rations. At Meertur, one of the largest camps, we were told by the Meertur mukhiya that food for the camp is population was provided for free by the government. People living in other camps told us that the government had provided free rations only up to August or September. By the time we visited these camps, only old people still got some rice a month, dal, potatoes and onions free. Living conditions in the camps are abysmal. We saw blanket distribution ceremonies in Gangaloor and Meertur camps, but little else to suggest that the government was interested in the welfare of the people staying in them. There is no proper shelter. People live in tents erected by the administration, or in little shacks made of plastic sheets and sticks that they have put up themselves. The tents were bare as people have few or no possessions. Sanitation and health conditions in the camps are very poor. Though we did see two health workers in Bhairamgarh camp, reports of Medicine Sans Frontiers suggest that health conditions in the camps are at crises levels. Some of the details of the Bhairamgarh camp highlighted by the CPI are open letter to the Prime Minister underline this situation: The camp is located close to the police station and the Bhairamgarh block headquarters. As many as 107 people from Sattuva village had been staying in a

5 × 16 metre space (less than 900 sq. feet) for three months. The administration gave no help in setting up the tents and people had to get sticks from the forest to build their tents. All the relief work was being done under the supervision of the administration and not through the local panchayat. People from camps were every now and then forced by the police to attend Salwa Judum rallies. One thing that bound people across camps was their anxiety as to whether they would ever be able to return home. Many people in camps would alternate between fear of Salwa Judum attacks and fear of Maoists while telling us about their reasons for being there. Many are there because of Salwa Judum attacks. There also prevails, among others, a vague fear of Maoist retaliation against those who join the Salwa Judum, willingly or under pressure, and then return to their villages. This fear is fuelled by the administration and Salwa Judum members, thus maintaining the pressure on people to keep living in camps, so much so that all outsiders not in uniform, like the fact-finding team, are viewed with suspicion. This is not all. The administration plans to make some of these camps permanent. (When we posed this question to the home secretary of Chhatisgarh he felt that while some may be able to return to their villages many may not be able to until such time as Maoists are not wiped out from the area.) About 200 people have been allotted land for houses along the highway in Kutru. This is part of the government's plan to create roadside villages, attached to police stations. While some of these villages may house people unable to return to their homes because of fear of Maoist retaliation the plan seems to be much wider in scope. Clearly, the government's agenda seems to be to empty out the villages, attack the Maoist mass base, and deny Maoists the food, shelter and other material support that enables the movement to function and grow. Salwa Judum leader Lakshman Kashyap admitted to having no idea about how people in these roadside villages would survive. Non-registration of FIRs and Atrocities by the Security Forces Combing operations and attacks on villages by the Naga IRB, CRPF and the Salwa Judum leave many people dead and injured. Almost all these killings are unrecorded. Apart from killings, the administration is arresting a number of people suspected of being Maoists or Maoist sympathisers. Most of these

detentions are completely illegal and unrecorded. This is not to mention the ill-treatment meted out to locals by the security forces stationed there. Whether it was a Naga soldier we spoke to or a CRPF officer, the sense of their superiority over the people they were meant to protect was overwhelming and shameful.

The people at the end of such treatment are those with absolutely no access to, and perhaps no knowledge of, legal aid. In a Jagdalpur hospital, we met two young girls, referred to as Naxalites by the nursės recovering from serious bullet injuries. One of them, Sambatti from Wanger village, refused to speak to us as she was either too scared or in too much pain to speak. The other, Phulmati, a resident of Belnar village, told us she had not been in touch with her family since she was arrested. She said she had been forcibly taken by some Maoists to harvest abandoned fields in Karkawada, near Nelasnar on the main highway just before Bhairamgarh. There were twenty of them including some members of a Maoist squad, working on the fields when police found them and opened fire at them. The Maoists returned fire. This led to the deaths of three boys, including two from Kodenar village, who died of police bullets. We found no record of the three boys deaths anywhere. We heard these boys have been buried in the grounds of Geedum police station. Whether this is true or not, this shows that the police are expected to commit the worst excesses. Sonia, an anganwadi worker in village Kamaloor was beaten, stripped and dragged by her hair and detained by some Naga IRB soldiers on 9th March. She is among the very few who have spoken up against the security forces. We could not meet her, but the mainstream media has covered her story. In Mankeli village, villagers said that they dared not go to the police station to file FIRs against the security forces for the five deaths that occurred there, fearing that they would be forced to live in camps and because they felt that the police had no interest in filing FIRs against their own crimes! There was no post mortem of those killed, the bodies were left in the village by the police and the last rites were performed by the villagers. This was reported to us in Kotarapal as well. The police only recorded crimes committed by the Maoists, and the district administration only maintained records of compensation paid to the victims of Maoist violence. A senior correspondent in Raipur told us that there is a government directive to keep silent over any killing by the Naga IRB. We could not confirm this, but the facts on the ground do indicate that non-registration of crimes by Salwa Judum and the security forces across Dantewada is a routine that this amounts to giving them carte blanche. Such selective recording of crimes also makes it appear that the only killings and violence are those committed by Maoists. This enables the government to fuel illfeeling against them and create an opinion in favour of a crackdown. In addition, such non-registration of FIRs in cases of killings by security forces denies compensation to the families of those killed. In an audio CD released by the Maoists to the Chhatisgarh press in August 2005, the SP Bijapur is heard complaining that the Jangla police station had foolishly allowed the deaths of two of the Maoists killed by the police in Kotarapal village to be incorrectly registered as killings by Maoists. Thus, he said, would allow the dead people's relatives to claim compensation, which in turn would be used to post bail for Naxalite sympathisers in jail. On the night of 30 November, while returning to Dantewada, we saw five people being loaded onto a truck.

Villagers told us that the Maoist Abujhmarh secretary had been arrested. We followed them to the Geedam police station where we met the detainees, which included two old and infirm people, a one-eyed man, and a young girl. They all said that they happened to be in Sattuva village, from where most people had already fled to camps. The river was in flood, one said, and they had been left behind because no more boats were available (boats had been stopped by the security forces for two days, as we discovered when we tried to cross the Indrâvati to reach Markapal village). He had an old mother, wife and three small children whom he had to take across. The girl said she had been grazing cattle when she was picked up. Another old man, a resident of Jhadka village, said he had come to stay with his brother in Sattuva and cultivate his fields there. They said they had been sitting in a house discussing how to go across the river when they were detained. The police claimed that these five had been arrested while possessing tiffin bombs the earlier evening

(29th November). There was no FIR showing the charges against them, let alone any arrest warrant. When we again visited Geedum police station on 1st December, the detainees complained that they had been beaten in custody. When we asked the station-in-charge whether an FIR had been filed, he said that the operation was still on, and they were waiting for it to conclude to register the FIR. This appears to be 27 Case of Kamlesh Paikra: Threat to Independent Journalists Kamlesh Paikra, 27, is a local journalist from Cherpal village, who till recently was working as Bijapur correspondent of Hindustan, when he fell afoul of the administration. Since he had been regularly reporting about the naxals in Dantewada, the SP Bijapur began to pressurise him about his naxal connections, and in April 2005, proposed that he reveal his sources to the police in complete violation of accepted journalistic practice the world over. When Kamlesh refused, the SP warned him of dire consequences. In September 2005, Salwa Judum gangs burnt down approximately 50 houses in Mankeli village, near Bijapur. There were unconfirmed reports of several deaths. Following Kamlesh's reporting of the, a CPI team visited Mankeli. After this, Kamlesh's harassment by the administration and Salwa Judum took a serious turn. In addition to being a journalist, Kamlesh ran a fair price shop in Bijapur. He used to buy rice from the Food Corporation of India at the BPL rate of Rs 5.70 a kilo and sell it at the saptahik bazaar for Rs 6.15. For this, he had to renew a permit every week. After his 8th September news report, first his quota of rice for the weekly bazaar was refused him. Then his permit was cancelled. No reason was given. Despite approaching the Food Inspector, the Assistant Collector, and the police, the permit was not renewed. His movement around Bijapur was also restricted. He was not allowed to visit the villages affected by Salwa Judum and the camps where displaced people are living. A PUCL team visited Dantewada between 26-29 November. They asked Kamlesh to accompany them; in spite of their presence, he was prevented from visiting the effected villages and camps. He was directly blamed for inviting both the CPI and the PUCL teams. Then they began to target his family. His elder brother Tarkeshwar Singh was a pabhari in Cherpal High School. The police claimed that naxal literature and uniforms were recovered from

Tarkeshwar's house and jailed him on 1st December, 2005. He was later charged in a bomb explosion case that happened in Padera village in which one jawan was injured. Tarkeshwar was released on bail two weeks later, but the case is still on. After further harassment, and fearing for his life, Kamlesh moved to Dantewada town in the third week of December with his wife and parents. He does not have a job or his fair price shop.

This seems to be the price for being an honest journalist. Kamlesh Paikra is a member of the Chhatisgarh Shramjivi Patrakar Sangh. They submitted an application on his behalf to the Chief Minister of Chhatisgarh, the Governor and the leader of the opposition. Nothing came of it. He is still afraid for his life. Kamlesh is not the only one. Another journalist, Lakshman Singh Kusram, also from Bijapur, reported on the molestation of some adivasi women by the CRPF jawans in Kutru. Now the police have reached his house, and have been threatening him. Shockingly, this violation of journalistic freedom is explicitly part of the administration's policy. The work plan of the Dantewada Collector maintains that there is need to institute restrictions on the media. This document argues that media coverage of Naxalite attacks makes it look as if they are gaining the upper hand. By reporting what the Naxalites are doing as against reporting how ordinary people are responding, the media indirectly gives the Naxalites a voice. It advocates controls on the media, beginning with a meeting between the administration and all news publishers/media channels reminding them of their accountability to the people.

The DSP, Dantewada also told us that FIRs showing arrests are recorded only when an operation concluded. When he was reminded that such delays in registering FIRs amounted to flouting the binding directive of the Supreme Court (in the D.K. Basu judgment) to record arrest within hours of detention, he claimed, shockingly, that in the midst of an undeclared war such delays are not unusual.

The Breakdown of Civil Administration: The civil administration is expected to be the interface between the people and the government. It is supposed to, apart from enforcing the policies and programmes of the government, act as a grievance redressal mechanism for ordinary people. It has not done that nor provided anything that can be seen as development for ordinary people. And due to the intensified conflict in recent times between the Maoists and the Salwa Judum, the police, which in theory is meant to be the civil institution for the prevention and detection of crime and the maintenance of rule of law, has become part of the war-like operations here, a euphemism for paramilitary formations. The situation we found in Dantewada has serious and frightening consequences for the formal functioning of democracy because the civil administration now operates on the whims of the Salwa Judum activists and the security forces, against common people. Although the District Collector assured us that our team members were free to move anywhere, it was apparent that on the highway (NH-16) the situation was different. While the CRPF or the Naga Battalion or the District Armed Police manned some checkpoints, it was even more disconcerting to note that Salwa Judum activists were manning their own checkpoints in full view of the government forces. They carried out searches of our vehicle and demanded to know the purpose of our visit. Salwa Judum members man checkpoints on roads, search people is belongings and control the flow of transport. We heard reports of how they had earlier been harassing bus drivers and had looted shops in Bijapur. The police simply look on at the checkpoints where Salwa Judum activists operate. While we were in Bijapur, Salwa Judum leaders kept walking into the SDM house and shouting at him for letting us visit the villages. The Salwa Judum made every effort to see that we did not go to Mankeli village. They also did not let us take local journalist Kamlesh Paikra with us. Also, the civilian population is being provided arms and training by the government, an alarming militarisation of civil society. At all the camps we visited between Geedam and Bijapur, namely Matwada, Bhairamgarh, Meertur, Nelasnar, Bijapur and Gangaloor, young men were undergoing training to become special police officers (SPOs). The SPOs, according to the Ditrict Collector and the station-in-charges Bhairamgarh and at Meertur, comprised either former sangham members or young adivasi men related to the Salwa Judum activists. It is not clear whether these SPOs will be provided guns or not are being set up and that some of these young men will become SPOs attached to VDCs. As mentioned,

SPOs under training have been promised Rs 1,500 per month, an honorarium set by central government for the SPOs as part of its counter-insurgency operations. We observed that some SPOs have been armed with guns, while bows and arrows have been distributed on a large scale to villages that join the Salwa Judum. The administration claims that these are the people's traditional weapons, but the collector's work plan makes it clear that distributing bows and arrow is part of the administration's plans (collector's Work Plan). All this calls into question the very notion of a civil administration; an administration that has failed to be accountable to the people is covering up its failures by co-opting common people. The local civil authority in Dantewada is unable to assert itself before the Salwa Judum activists.

The Background Dantewada

Region and its People: Dantewada district, situated at the southern tip of Chhatisgarh, has borders with Maharashtra, Andhra Pradesh and Orissa and was part of Bastar kingdom till 1947. After independence, it was merged with Kanker kingdom to form Bastar, the largest district (39,114 sq km) in the state of Madhya Pradesh. In 1998, Bastar was divided into three districts, Kanker, Bastar and Dantewada, and in 2001 all three district became part of the newly formed state of Chhatisgarh. Recently, Bijapur has been carved out as a new police district in Dantewada. With a population of 7.91 lakh, Dantewada district has the lowest population density in the state at 40.8 persons per square kilometer (2001, census). Topographically, the region is composed of an undulating plateau, with hill ranges cut by a number of rivulets that flow into the Indrâvati River. These riverbeds provide the space for most rural settlements. Godavari and Mahanadi are two major rivers that arise from the Bastar uplands. The district is divided into four tehsils: Bhopal patnam, Bijapur, Dantewada and Konta. The Salwa Judum and police operations originated in Bijapur tehsil, but have now spread to Konta. The people inhabiting the district are predominantly tribal, mostly Maria Gonds and Dorla accounting for 82 per cent of the rural population. Scheduled Castes account for about three per cent of 788 the population and the rest are OBC communities like the Sundis, Kallars etc.

A number of immigrants, mostly traders, but also lower level officials, school teachers, health workers etc., have settled in the small market towns like Bijapur, Sukma, Konta and Dantewada. The Bailadilla mines hardly employed any local adivasis, with the result that the mining town of Kirandul is a non-tribal enclave, with little connection to the surrounding countryside. This picture of a large number of fairly small tribal villages, and a few large villages, with on-tribal households is supported by the census data. Of the 1220 villages in the district, 455 are wholly tribal and another 458 are more than 90 per cent tribal, i.e., 75 per cent of the districts villages are almost completely tribal. Only 76 villages, or approximately six per cent of the two larger villages serve as local markets and it is these that tend to have greater non-tribal populations. About 38 per cent of the rural area in the district is outside the village and part of forest land. The 2001 Census states these forests have 202 villages, of which about 90 are inhabited. What is pertinent is that these villages have no land rights and are at the mercy of the forest department. Dantewada has one National Park (Indravati) and two wildlife sanctuaries (Bhairamgarh and Pamed)]. Other than these, the rest of the villages occupy 62 per cent of the district, but again 46 per cent of this is also designated as forest. Hence in total, about two-thirds of the district belongs to the Forest Department, at least on paper. Some of these forest areas may have been village lands earlier. For instance, in the areas under the Bhopalpatnam and Kutru zamindaris, feudal oppression during colonial times forced residents to flee their villages. After 1947 and the abolition of Zamindari, these residents came back to find their lands notified as forests. The villagers are heavily dependent on both agriculture and forests. Of the total village land, barely 29 per cent land is cultivated, and as said earlier, nearly half is designated as forest and the rest is either uncultivable or is culturable waste. The average landholding per household (2001 Census) works out to 1.01 hectare, i.e., 2.5 acres. Irrigation being by and large absent (barely two per cent have some sort of irrigation), only a single crop is possible. The shifting of villages due to economic reasons is therefore common. In the 2001 Census, there are 30 such villages that have become uninhabited (this is in addition to 112 uninhabited forest villages).

Some of these villages continue to practice shifting cultivation in forest areas, a practice that has been banned by the government, except in the Abujhmarh areas to the north of the Indravati. The land actually under cultivation may be significantly more than these figures suggest. Villagers have cleared significant areas designated as forest land within the village for cultivation. Most of the people own land, thus 84 per cent of the main workers in rural Dantewada and 55 per cent of the marginal workers are cultivators. Yet, the paucity of land, and the low yields forces six per cent of the main workers and 39 per cent of the marginal workers to work as agricultural labour (in all, around 14 per cent of the total working population). Such employment is provided on the lands of those who own larger and/or more fertile plots. They work either as Naukar, i.e., free labour obtaining a seasonal wage, or as kabadi, i.e., attached labour with a larger landowner, getting food in lieu of wages. Such sale and purchase of labour is concentrated in some villages while being wholly absent in most others. Of the district's 1,220 villages, nearly 400 have no agricultural labourers and in all nearly 800 villages have less than 10 per cent, while 96 villages have more than 50 per cent agricultural labour. Labourers also migrate to neighbouring areas in Andhra Pradesh and Maharashtra for work. Given the rain-fed agriculture, the collection and sale of non-timber forest produce at weekly haats (markets) or to agents is an important source of local income, a fact that underlines the people is dependence on the forest, and their forced interaction with Forest Department officials and traders. At the village level, authority and respect is commanded by the Patel/pedda/mukhia (headman) and the priest. In some cases, the same person performed both functions. The next rung in the structure is the pargan manjh the head of a cluster of villages, a person of considerable clout. The headmen, in many instances, belong to households that are the oldest residents of the village, or those who initially set up in the village.

The process of the shifting of populations led to later settlements within existing revenue villages, with the newer settlers obtaining lower amounts of land and less productive lands in comparison to the earlier settlers. Thus, while cultural practices ensure that economic differences are not visible in dress and size of dwelling, the older practice of collective labour has now become a means of garnering the labour of the less well-off by those better-off. Literacy levels are low in rural areas at 29 per cent for men and 14 per cent for women, with an overall rural literacy rate of 21 per cent. Yet this presents apartial picture. In Bijapur tehsil for instance, there are only 52 villages in which more than 25 per cent of the population is literate, and 35 villages have no literates at all. This is related to the availability and the quality of schools in the district: out of the 1220 villages, 214 do not have even a primary school and, of these, for 107 villages the school is more than five kilometers away. The presence of a school building in the village, moreover, does not ensure that teachers are available. In some cases, teachers use the excuse of the presence of Maoist organisations in the village to remain absent. In any case, with the ongoing Salwa Judum, schools have come under attack. Security forces have been using school buildings as temporary camps and Maoists have been blasting these buildings to prevent security forces from finding pucca shelters in the villages. The situation is distinctly worse regarding health facilities. Out of the 1220 villages, there is no medical facility in 1161 villages. A primary health center exists only in 26 villages; a private registered medical practitioner in 17 villages, a government subsidised one in 12 and a community health worker in 122 villages. A telling comment on the inadequacy of the health infrastructure and the health and well being of the people is provided through the studies conducted by Chhatisgarh PUCL in earlier years. As early as 1987, an investigation into repeated reports of blood dysentery in Bastar that claimed many lives each year revealed that people had very limited access to potable water. A more recent study during 2004 revealed that things had not really improved very much in the last 18 years, gaps in physical and social infrastructure for a period of just one year. For the construcopment is to provide Rs 37.5 crore per annum for naxal-affected areas under the Prime Minister's Grameen Swarojgar Yojana (PMGSY).

Indeed, what passes for development in official parlance has a security imprint. The physical infrastructure to be built includes other than police stations roads, bridges, etc. While roads, bridges and electrification will no doubt benefit ordinary people, it is evident that their needs are hardly what are behind the bringing in of the Border Roads Organisation for building roads in the region. An official Work Proposal from the Collector's office states that the real rationale of road building and widening is to flush the Maoists out from the jungles and make troop movement in the area easier. The BRO road from Jagdalpur to Dantewada, for instance, is not being built through the panchayats, and thus does not even provide local employment. To summarise, the adivasis and other local inhabitants of the region have little possibility of actual development and are acutely aware of their marginal and exploited status. For the overwhelming majority in the villages, agriculture is unviable since plots are small and there is no investment in irrigation, there are severe restrictions on the use of forests partly due to the creation of wildlife reserves, the prices of forest produce are deliberately kept low by traders and the government, and the government machinery treats them with apathy and contempt. On the other hand, there is a small minority, mostly trading families, shopkeepers, members of the bureaucracy, lawyers and others living in the small towns, and some rich tribal leaders who have gained through politics or corruption involving illicit felling of trees who want large development projects. In a situation where the state claims rights to the land and the people who live on that land are treated as peripheral to the national economy, a mass base of the Maoists challenging this status quo forms a threat to the state's plans for heavy industry and profits in this region. Political Movements the first political mobilisation in the former Bastar district under the aegis of a political party took place in the mid-1970s, by the Communist Party of India (CPI). It created its organisation in the Bailadilla mines, around issues of control over mineral resources and work opportunities for locals. The struggle in the mines was brutally suppressed through state repression, including police firing on protesting workers during 1976-77 that resulted in the death of several workers and members of their families. The movement begun by the CPI spread through large areas of Bastar and brought the party electoral success in two of the three legislative assembly seats.

The other issues taken up by them centred around the lack of amenities and access to forests. The CPI had for long demanded an India Reserve Battalions.

The Government of India raises one or more India Reserve Battalions [IRBs] in each state. The concept of IRBs was mooted by the Ministry of Home Affairs in the background of increasing problems of law and order and emerging internal security scenario in the country, which put considerable pressure on the Central Police Forces. As of 2004-05, there were 85 IRBs in the country, each having 1,007 personnel. These battalions are trained by the CRPF and the BSF in fighting with modern weaponry. The responsibility for recruiting and maintaining these battalions rests with the state governments, but the central government bears the expenses towards raising and training its personnel. However, the central government has the power to deploy the IRBs anywhere on payment to the concerned state. *Source:* Ministry of Home Affairs 2004-05. Autonomous council for the Bastar area to ensure a degree of independence in the formulation and implementation of development policy. Movements against the dominant development paradigm and rampant corruption in the administration continued throughout the 1980s and 1990s. Many of these were local in character. These included the movement against pine forestation to feed the Ballarshah Paper Industries, the movement of the women of Asna near Jagdalpur against forest enclosure and monoculture forestry, and the resistance of the tribals of Mawlibhata to a proposed steel plant on their land. In recent times, the most serious challenge to the dominant model of development has come from the CPI (Maoist) formations.

Naxal Affected Area in India

The state's central approach towards this challenge focuses mainly so far on the reestablishment of law and order. Since the general elections during spring 2009 the situation aggravated, especially after the Indian government started a comprehensive offensive called Operation Green Hunt, deploying around 70,000 paramilitary troops against the Naxalites. This year nearly 800 people have been killed in the conflict so far. Almost daily the media report about the clashes between Naxalites and security forces. Due to its complexity the conflict is often presented in a simplified manner in the public discourse. Surprisingly this conflict receives a very low degree of international attention, although it is one of the biggest internal armed conflicts in the world. In this regard this paper wants to be a corrective. The intention is to give an extensive overview on the topic of Naxalism in India for interested readers whether in India or abroad without neglecting the complexity of the topic. Despite the fact that the issue exists since more than 40 years, relatively little research work has been conducted. However, within recent years a rapid increase in academic work can be observed that is dealing with the roots and causes of Naxalism.

The programme of the CPI(Maoist), once the new people's democratic state is established, however, is one with which 'a large chunk of the Indian political class should have nothing to quarrel about'. The party proposes to redistribute land to poor peasants and landless labourers according to the slogan 'land to the tillers'; to ensure the land rights of women; 'to ensure all facilities for the growth of agriculture', including ensuring 'remunerative prices' for agricultural products'; to regulate working conditions and ensure that wages are adequate and equal between the sexes; to guarantee the right to work and 'improved living conditions for the people'; and 'to move towards the elimination of regional imbalances'. Much of this also appears in the Common Minimum Programme with which the United Progressive Alliance (UPA), headed by the Congress Party, set out (also in 2004), while the major established party of the Left, the CPI(M), remains committed to the abolition of landlordism and radical land reforms. They are now seen increasingly as being more or less exclusively an armed movement with no concern for mass mobilisation has come about because state action against them leaves them with little scope for the latter, which has tended to shrink or at least apparently. The chances of land reform being carried out in India by intervention from above now seem remote. Neither is there significant pressure for such reforms from below in the major agricultural regions of the country. It has been argued that 'the main reason for the wide popularity of the Naxalites in the entire forest region abutting the Godavari river in Telangana, Vidarbha and Chhatisgarh is the protection they gave to the forest dwellers for cultivation in reserve forests, the substantial increase they achieved in the payment for picking tendu leaf and the end they put to the oppressive domination of the headmen and patwaris'. The massive transfers of forest and agricultural land for infrastructural, mining and industrial projects that are either planned or are now taking place will lend even greater strength to the Naxalites.

Tactics, Mobilisations and Patterns of Support

The few ethnographic studies that there are 51 strongly confirm these general arguments about the extent to which the Naxalites win support amongst and articulate the needs and aspirations of poor and landless peasants and adivasis, and perhaps especially of young men and women. The studies that I have found in addition to my studies are those of Bela Bhatia in Central Bihar, of George Kunnath, also in Central Bihar, 'Becoming a Naxalite in Rural Bihar: Class Struggle and its Contradictions', Journal of Peasant Studies, Vol. 33, No.1 (January 2006), pp. 89-123 and 'Smouldering Dalit Fires in Bihar, India', Dialectical Anthropology, Vol. 33, Nos. 3-4 (2009), pp. 309-325; of Alpa Shah, in Jharkhand, 'Markets of Protection The "Terrorist" Maoist Movement and the State in Jharkhand, India', Critique of Anthropology, Vol. 26, No. 3 (2006), and 'In search of certainty in revolutionary India', Dialectical Anthropology, Vol. 33, Nos. 3-4 (2009), pp. 271-286; of Amit Desai, in Maharashtra, "Anti-witchcraft" and the Maoist insurgency in rural Maharashtra, India', Dialectical Anthropology, Vol. 33, Nos. 3-4 (2009), pp. 423-439; and of Jason Miklian, in Chhatisgarh, *op. cit*. The work of Felix Padel on tribal movements in Central India, some of which is available on line, is also of value, as are reports of enquiry teams from the Peoples Union for Civil Liberties (PUCL) and other bodies of this kind. This is so even if they actually enter a region through the rural middle class of upper caste elites and educated well-to-do adivasis, as has been the case in the part of Jharkhand studied by Alpa Shah. These studies also, however, highlight the tensions and contradictions in the tactics and actions of the movements. The relationship between the mainly urban, educated middle class leadership and the peasantry is fraught with tensions. There are contradictions between the immediate tactics of the groups, of opposing the dominant, Landowners, redistributing land, raising wages and generally of changing rural power relations, all of which answers to the problems that their supporters confront and on the other hand, their longer run goals of establishing socialism through the take-over of state power. It seems from the ethnographies that, unsurprisingly, the extent to which the leadership has been able to develop a 'revolutionary consciousness' amongst the poor peasantry is very limited. George Kunnath's research in particular, shows how support amongst Dalits for the Maoists in Central Bihar weakened considerably, as the latter sought to bring in men from the middle and upper castes in pursuit of the goal of capturing state power and rewarded the higher caste members of their armed squads (*dastas*) more highly than the Dalits. The tendency on the part of the leadership to romanticise the revolutionary character of the peasantry is sometimes a problem and it is clear that such as this consciousness is, it may well be suppressed when government provides adequately for the most immediate needs of the people. The other big tension is between mass mobilisation and the necessarily secretive, armed power of the underground movement which is not inherently democratic at all. This relates in turn to the contradiction between the moral basis of the Maoist movement and the violence that it perpetrates. Violence can undermine that moral base and alienate supporters as has happened, according to Balagopal's account – summarised earlier – in Andhra Pradesh. The understandable sense of their persecution amongst Maoist cadres, confronted by the violence of the state, may lead to the indiscriminate use of force and their alienation from the people they claim to fight for. It is clear, too, and also unsurprising that there is but a thin line between the 'revolutionary' and the criminal thug. One of the early leaders in Central Bihar (one of a pair referred to colloquially as 'Marx and Engels') was a Yadav dacoit who had served a long prison sentence for the murder of a police constable. Bhatia and Kunnath provide ethnographic evidence that the social base of the Movement in Central Bihar, when the Movement was strong there, was amongst the landless, small and marginal peasants of lower and intermediate castes, though there were some supporters from amongst higher castes and classes and whose presence was felt in the leadership. These authors show that there was a perception amongst poorer people that Naxalites were 'good people', who Sumanta Banerjee argues this in his 2009 article. Balagopal 2006, says with regard to Andhra Pradesh 'strategies of militancy attract unruly were opposed to their oppressors and who supported them in a struggle for their basic rights. But according to Bhatia, people understood the objective of the movement as being 'change', not 'revolution'. They supported it because they felt that the Naxalites shared their sense of injustice rather than for any ideological reasons. The appeal of 'class struggle' was as a means of securing needs for higher wages, land redistribution and freedom from harassment. Bhatia notes that people petitioned the Maoists for exactly the same things for which they also petitioned government. Bhatia describes mobilisations by Dalits against Bhumihar landowners in Bhojpur; Kunnath the struggles between Maoist-led landless Dalits and Kurmi landholders in another village in Central Bihar.

In both cases, the accounts show that the 'feudal' power of the landowners was undermined but at a high cost in terms of human life. In this region, of course, the Maoists began to be opposed in the 1990s by vigilante gangs set up by the landowners, like the Bhumihars' Ranbeer Sena. Still, the ethnographies show that the Maoist mobilisations delivered some real benefits to landless peasants. They established land rights for some, raised wages in the areas of struggle and perhaps above all, inspired poor people to assert themselves as human beings and to claim their social and political rights. 'Honour' or 'self-respect' appears for many to have been their most important achievement from their participation in the mass mobilisations of the Maoists. In practice, Bhatia argues on the basis of extensive fieldwork in Central Bihar in the mid-1990s, a large part of the Movement's activities were non-violent (demonstrations, dharnas and the like). Still, there were significant differences between Liberation (castigated by General Secretary Ganapathy as having degenerated 'after a history of glorious struggle'), Party Unity and the MCC over the extent of their commitment to the mass line represented by the open fronts set up by the various groups. Liberation formed the Indian People's Front (IPF) and the Bihar Pradesh Kisan Sabha (BPKS) in the early 1980s and both flourished. Party Unity set up the Mazdoor Kisan Sangram Samiti

(MKSS) was banned in 1986 but was later renamed Mazdoor Kisan Sangram Parishad (MKSP) but underground, armed action was always important. At the outset and again more recently according to other commentators, the groups relied almost exclusively on armed tactics. These were undertaken by the *dasta* (squads), each with 6-10 members recruited mostly locally from amongst the labouring classes, though they might also include middle class members, some from outside the area. The most important role of the dasta, according to Bhatia, was (in the 1990s) to protect the open fronts; open fronts and underground groups were intimately linked. Kunnath records that they were referred to always together as this description appears in 'Interview with Ganapathy'. Kunnath 2009, analyses the tensions that eventually emerged between Party Unity and the MKSS, and the split in the latter. His account, from fieldwork undertaken more recently than Bhatia's, shows that the squads increasingly included middle class and middle caste members as the Maoists sought to build a wider cross-class movement in the pursuit of the goal of securing state power. His friend Rajubhai, a landless Dalit who had been the leader of a dasta and who appears to be an organic intellectual, told him that: When the sanghathan came here, it began among the *mazdoor varg* (working class). The cadres used to sleep and eat in the mud houses of the mazdoor. It fought for the issues of the working classes – land and wages, as well as against social abuses, exploitation and sexual abuse of women. But now that the sanghathan has got a foothold here, its ambition has grown into one of capturing state power.

So, they have started taking in people from dominant castes, against whom we fought previously. As a result of the entry of the landowning castes into the sanghathan, it is hesitant to raise the issues of land and wages. For the last twenty years, wages have remained the same: three kilos of paddy for a day's work. The working class is no longer a priority for the sanghathan. Rajubhai's disaffection from the sanghathan was completed by the fact that landless Dalits in the dastas, though they were the ones who died or suffered physically the most, were actually paid less than were the middle caste members. This appears to be a rather shocking denial of the moral claims of the Movement. A village study from South Bihar by Shashi Bhushan Singh presents a more complex, even confusing picture, though it also bears out some of the points made by Bhatia and Kunnath. Here it appears that the IPF, the open front of Liberation and the MKSS of Party Unity – though they were both led locally mainly by Yadavs – were a source of support for Dalits in their struggles against higher castes for higher wages and for their dignity. Singh says, 'The biggest contribution of the Naxalites towards the empowerment of the poor has been the taming of the upper castes'. These struggles took place, however, in a context in which the traditional dominance of Rajputs had already been weakened by the effects of economic development. This, in various ways, drew people increasingly out of the village. By the later 1990s, Dalit support for the Naxalites was apparently waning, mainly because of the improvements that had taken place in the Dalits' economic condition and perhaps also because the class contradiction between the landed and landless had by then become less clear-cut: 'The importance of land as a factor of livelihood and dominance is decreasing the locus of the economy has partially shifted Kunnath 2006, Singh, 'Limits to Power: Naxalism and Caste Relations in a South Bihar Village', No. 29 (16 July, 2005), away from the village'. The politics of Maoism in this case were greatly influenced by caste and its implications for the wider political realignments that took place in Bihar in the 1990s. The Dalit's themselves were divided by class differences (mainly between the Chamars and the rest); many of the Yadavs shifted politically to become supporters of Lalu Prasad Yadav's Rashtriya Janata Dal (RJD); while the MCC had entered the region later than the other groups and through upper caste Bhumihars and Rajputs, and finally became closely associated with the latter when the Bhumihars opposed to Lalu and the RJD; also shifted to become the main opposition to the Maoists through the Ranbeer Sena. In this case, 'The MCC supported Rajputs and opposed the Scheduled Castes initially in order to gain supremacy vis-à-vis the MKSS and later for survival vis-à-vis the police and Ranvir Sena. An organisation formed to support the Scheduled Castes ended up by supporting the dominant castes'. The neatness of class conflict is completely upset in this case and no doubt, the same is true of many other areas. While it may be true, as it is according to the close observers of the Movement in Central Bihar whose work has been referred to here, that revolutionary violence can appeal to these who have been subjected to violence by their social 'superiors' over generations, Bhatia particularly – like Banerjee – is clearly deeply concerned about the way in which violence corrupts the Movement. Her conclusion – with which, I believe, Kunnath's arguments are in sympathy – is worth quoting in full: The Naxalite movement will thrive only to the extent that its vision resonates with the people. The wider the gap between the two, the higher the chances the movement will fizzle out.

The present formula is a mélange of convenience between the leaders who dream of Maoist revolution and people who aspire for practical change. In order to bring about a genuine people's movement, the Naxalite leaders have to be ready to walk at the pace of the people and let their concerns guide the vision of the movement. The story of the Movement in Andhra Pradesh according to Balagopal, as recounted earlier, is salutary. There, he argues, the gap between the visions of leadership and masses has seriously weakened the Movement. The leadership has the commitment to 'armed struggle' that is explained in the Party Programme while the Maoists are also subjected to such violence by the state that both sides have become locked into armed conflict. (Bela Bhatia, *'On Armed Resistance'*, Economic and Political Weekly, Vol. XLI, No. 29 (22 July, 2006), and Sumanta Banerjee 2006.) Bhatia writes '...the use of violence has taken a heavy toll. The downside of violence has been so wide-ranging that it may well end up negating what the Naxalites stand for, experiences, for notable example, of the attempts in Andhra Pradesh to reach a negotiated settlement have shown just how difficult this is to achieve given the legitimate suspicions of the Maoists of the government and vice versa. Thus far there are no ethnographic studies of the Movement in the Bastar region of Chhatisgarh to compare with those for Central Bihar, though Nandini Sundar who has carried on substantial ethnographic research in the region – if not in the Maoist dominated areas, as she says – has written on it, drawing on interviews conducted as part of a Citizens' Initiative visit there in May 2006. Her information about the activities of Salwa Judum (discussed below) is substantiated by interviews and observations in the field reported by Jason Miklian. Sundar records that the Maoists 'claim to include 60 lakh (60,00,000) people in the "organisational sweep" of their Dandakaranya "guerilla zone"', where they have established mass organisations – the most important of which are the Dandakaranya Adivasi Kisan Mazdoor Sanghathan (DAKMS) and the Krantikari Adivasi Mahila Sanghathan (KAMS) – that are colloquially called sanghams.

The Maoists claim, also, to have carried on a great deal of developmental work, including the establishment of 135 people's clinics, educational facilities and a large number of minor irrigation works. Sundar comments that while these efforts – assuming that the Maoists' claims are accurate – are not equivalent to what the government might have achieved, they do show much greater commitment to people's development. The KAMS is said to have taken up women's issues and the Maoists have consciously promoted Gondi language and literature. These positive efforts, however, are eight 'resisted even genuine government initiatives'. For example, 'While recognising that traders cheat adivasis over minor forest produce, (the Maoists) have defended them against government attempts to introduce cooperatives to buy tamarind and tendu'. Miklian, too, comments that most villagers 'are upset at Naxal opposition to government programmes and efforts to block participatory elections'. More significant still, than this, has been the 'brute force' that has accompanied their work. Sundar argues, 'Their supporters need to debate whether armed struggle was necessary to their positive work and whether peaceful mass mobilisation would not work on the Andhra peace talks (see K. Balagopal, 'People's War and the Government: did the police have the last laugh?', Economic and Political Weekly, Vol. XXXVIII (8th February 2003); and 'Naxalites in Andhra Pradesh: Have We Heard the Last of the Peace Talks?', Economic and Political Weekly, Vol. XLV (26th March, 2005), Nandini Sundar, 'Bastar, Maoism and Salwa Judum', Economic and Political Weekly, Vol. XLI, No. 29 (22nd July 2006), pp. 3187-92; and Miklian 2009. See also Arundhati Roy's account, op. cit. and Sundar's contribution, 'Pleading for justice', Seminar, March 2010. Sundar, *Ibid*, p. 3189.

Arundhati Roy, op. cit., also gives some account of the developmental work undertaken by the Maoists; and see Balagopal 2006,op. cit. (note 50), on the reasons for the mass support that the Maoists have attracted. Arundhati Roy, *op. cit.*, describes activities of the KAMS. Better certainly, the attempt to defend their guerilla zone seems now to have overtaken people's needs. Her conclusion then is exactly like Bhatia's from Bihar or Balagopal's from Andhra. Gautam Navlakha gives a somewhat more sympathetic account of the Maoists in Bastar from the journey he made in their 'base area' there, where they run their Jantanam Sarkar or 'people's government' in January 2010. He, likes Arundathi Roy was evidently very impressed by the self-discipline of the young cadres amongst whom he observed remarkable gender equality. He notes the large numbers of women and that many platoons of the People's Liberation Guerilla Army have women commanders. He says, 'It is significant that women comprise by far and away the most articulate members of the movement' and records its work to encourage (not 'decree') the emancipation of women as also to develop education, healthcare and agricultural production. According to Navlakha's account, the Maoists are very concerned indeed to explain and defend their policy in regard to violence. They point to the violence that is carried on against the people quite routinely by police and private militia of the Salwa Judum and strongly assert that only 'enemies of the people' were killed by them. This defence was also articulated forcefully by General Secretary Ganapathy in his interview with Myrdal and Navlakha, and by the Jharkhand leader Gopalji, interviewed by Alpa Shah. But it is clear that there is a great deal of sensitivity amongst the Maoist leadership about undisciplined violence. Navlakha says, 'I pointed out that each time the party committed a mistake and apologised, it could not help advance the movement forward. Did not this raise issues about discipline?'

This line of questioning clearly discomfited those with whom he spoke. There can be no doubt that there is a spiral of violence as Bhatia and others show. At the same time, the police who are set against the Maoists come from what Human Rights Watch has described as a 'broken system': 'A dangerous anachronism, the police have largely failed to evolve from the ruler supportive, repressive forces they were designed to be under Britain's colonial rule ... Instead of policing through public consent and participation, the police use abuse and threats as a primary crime investigation and law enforcement tactic. The institutional culture of police practically discourages officers from acting otherwise, failing to give them the resources, training, ethical environment and encouragement to develop professional police tactics. Many officers even told Human Rights Watch that they were ordered or expected to commit abuses'. (Human Rights Watch, Broken System: Dysfunction, Abuse and Impunity in the Indian Police (New York: Human Rights Watch, 2009).) There are some other points that emerge from the little ethnography. One interesting finding is that of Amit Desai from his fieldwork in one of the two Naxalite affected districts of Maharashtra. Here the presence of the Maoists has had the effect of bringing the police, moved into 'advanced bases', closer to village people. Aware as they now are of the need to 'win hearts and minds', the police sometimes provide support for villagers in their interactions with other bodies of the state. But they are also convinced that 'social backwardness' is a major reason why people may support the Maoists. With this mindset, the police have attempted at a kind of social reform by trying to regulate local religious practice and such activities as witch-detecting and ghost-finding. This has had the consequence, in this case, of pushing people into closer involvement with the alternative religious practice offered by a particular Hindu sect that is aligned with the Hindu right. The Maoists have generally been silent in regard to the increasing influence that Hindu nationalists have sought to build amongst tribal. Sumanta Banerjee writes that 'their major failure has been their powerlessness in putting up an effective resistance to the Hindu religious fascist forces which have imposed a reign of terror over members of the Muslim and Christian religious minorities.

The sense of in security confusion and dilemma have been observed in the above pages among the activist, academician, intellectual, Naxalites, Maoist, policy-makers, planners, administrators, and it is persisting. So long the clarity of the problem and the solution. does not come to each stake holders, the solution is a far cry. In the above pages I have quoted some of the views expressed by different experts also in order to bring clarity and continuity on the subject in the interest of the problem of internal security and development of the people living in the tribal region of the country.

In the forthcoming pages I have discussed the currents scenario of Chhatisgarh and Jharkhand. In the beginning the 'Peace Dialogue Initiative by Social Scientists' have been discussed and in the next section 'The Naxalism and Maoism in Jharkhand' in the perspective of Tana Bhagat have been discussed.

Section—A

Peace Dialogue Initiative by Social Scientists and Independent Citizens in Bastar Area of Chhatisgarh

Introduction

The area of Bastar is inhabited by the Gond tribals. The sub-castes of the Gonds that inhabit the area are the Maria, Muria and Dorla as well as a small group, which call themselves the Raj Gonds. The three other tribal groups that inhabit Bastar are Bhatra, Dhurva and Halba. The Gonds are, by and large, simple people who have been living in the area doing primitive agriculture, collecting minor forest produce, forging metal artifacts, fishing and hunting. The Gonds have a primitive religion on which there has been a superimposition of Hindu Goddess, Danteshwari (Shakti). However, their primitive Gods still exist and are worshipped. Gonds indulge in fertility rites and other similar symbolic rites. Divorces, remarriages, widow marriages, marriages with the wives of brothers are common. In earlier times, marriages between brothers and sisters were also allowed but this tradition has dwindled in most parts of Bastar. In all the sub-castes of Gonds, the bridal price has to be paid by the groom. The Gond tribals of Bastar also have their own ghotul system that, in fact, was the common dormitory where mature boys and girls live to participate in dancing, singing, story telling, etc. Additionally, Ghotuls were places where the young Gond (both male and female) learnt his tribal education of relationships and hierarchies including social behaviour in simulated atmosphere of a village hierarchy. The education also included practical sex education. Only unmarried men and women were allowed to live in Ghotuls. While this institution has dwindled among other sub-tribes, the Muria Gonds still continue with this system. The Marias are divided between the Abhuj Maria and Bison Horn Maria. The Abhuj Maria live in the hill tracks of Abhuj Mar. They were very simple people living in isolation and avoiding the outer world. Their only contact with the outer world was to barter their gold (which they use to pan) and forest produce for salt. For a long time, the government had decided not to disturb them and it was for this reason the Abhuj Mar area has not been surveyed so far. The Bison Horn Maria, on the other hand, lived in the south of Indrawati river in the plains or lower hill formations. They wear Bison horns as headgear in their dancing rituals. The Murias are another sub-caste/sub-tribe of Gonds and they mostly inhabit in Narainpur and Kondagaon tehsil of Bastar district. All tribals are simple people. Their economy is mainly based on agriculture and collection of minor forest produce. They have no functional division of caste like barbers, cobblers, weaver, washermen, sweepers, etc. While all the tribals in the past did shifting cultivation, most of them have started practicing sedentary and fixed cultivation systems. All the tribals drink Mahua liquor and toddy of Sago-Palm Tree, called 'Sulfie'.

Most of the tribals have several totems and several Gods that include Gods of the villages, tribal sub-groups and even Gods to protect various Institutions like the Ghotuls. There is a fair degree of superstition among the tribals of Bastar and various magic rites for healing etc. These medicine men or witch doctors are called Sirhas and hold very important position in the village hierarchy. Most tribal villages have their own headmen whom they respect and their own tribal panchayats (which is different from the elected panchayats). Though the above description of Bastar tribal would make one think that the Bastar tribal is a very simple and peace loving person, the fact is that because of this innate simplicity his mind functions in a very simplistic arc of love and peace on the one side and hatred and violence on the other. Verrier Elvin in his work 'Maria Murders and Suicides' had clearly shown through various case studies that the tolerance threshold to physical and emotional pain of a Maria tribal is very low and he would kill or commit suicide for smallest of reasons. Interestingly, Elvin does not talk of the Bastar tribals as a group responding violently to a real or perceived pain although there have been incidences of such violent response also. For example, in 1876 the tribals of Bastar had risen in revolt against outsiders and foreigners and had started arson and killings that had to be brutally suppressed. In 1910, there was another revolt. In a confidential letter No. 60, dated 29th March, 1910 of the General Provincial Administration (Political and Military Deptt.) B.P. Standan, Esq., C.L.E., I.C.S., Chief Secretary to the Chief Commissioner, Central Provinces wrote to the Secretary to the Government of India, Political Department, Simla indicating the nature, dimension and virulence of violence perpetuated by the tribals. He also states that the list of grievances obtained from a tribal rebel of Bastar.

Researchers in Dantewada

The Points Reveal:

1. Inclusion of village land in Reserve Forest;
2. High-handed treatment and unjust exactions on the part of forest officials;
3. Maltreatment of pupils as well as their parents by village school teachers to extract money and eatables in order to purchase supplies/arrange food for Tehsildars and inspectors;
4. Forcible purchase by school village masters for food supply at 1/4th of the market price and similar acts by police

employees in addition to Beggar, and beating up of tribals to compel cheap supply of grains, etc.

5. Exaction of excessive Begari by Malgujars;
6. Interference with the right of manufacturing intoxicating liquors;
7. Practice of officials getting houses built through Begari;
8. Exactions by the lessees of villages on account of which the people asked that they may be allowed to pay both land revenue and forest dues directly (instead of through Malgujars);
9. General operations of various kinds on the part of officials.

The interesting point in this letter was that B.P. Standan agreed that the grievances were genuine but pointed out that to excuse their violence would lead to similar repetitions of violence on even petty issues. He, however, did state that extension of organised government among the tribals 'needed greater circumspection, and control over subordinate officials must be the closest if legitimate cause of grievance was to be avoided'. The letter also debunked the belief that the forest can only be protected by forest officials and stated that 'forests can be reasonably protected even among a Maria population as has been demonstrated by the successful management of forest of the large Ahiri Jamindari which borders the 'Bastar State'. The fact remains that the reality of the tribal situation in Bastar did not change much after Independence. From the point of view of tribals in Bastar, their poverty arises directly out of the state policy towards the forest. When the first reservation of forest was undertaken by then princely state of Bastar in 1910, it led to rebellion as stated above. That rebellion could only be suppressed with the help of the Indian Army. After coming into force of the Indian Forest Act after Independence, the tribal was granted certain rights in the forest. Owing to large-scale ignorance of these rights among the tribals, they were more often than not denied these rights by lower foreign functionaries. They were often harassed and threatened that they would be dispossessed of their land in the forest villages leading to a very strained relationship between the tribals and the forest department. With the declaration of a large area in Bijapur as Indrawati

National Park, many of the forest villages falling within its precincts had to be evacuated leading to extreme distress among the tribals. The exploitation of iron-ore rich Dantewada by the NMDC continues to remain atraumatic experience for tribals of Bastar. In Dantewada tehsil, there are around 200-300 odd children who have no place in tribal society. They are the children of various officers, engineers and men who worked in Bailadila complex during its excavation/construction period from tribal mothers. The then Collector of Bastar, Dr B.D. Sharma, had forced some of these men to marry the tribal girls whom they had sexually exploited, but today, not one of them is around to support the children. Most of these sexually exploited Adivasi girls were forced into prostitution. The tribal allergy to exploitation of minerals in Bastar stems from this sad experience. Despite Nehru's insistence on gradual integration of tribals into the national mainstream culture and a series of enlightened bureaucrats who worked as Collector, Bastar and tried to ensure not to affect the tribal systems in a traumatic manner, most of the bureaucrats at the lower, middle and senior levels of the districts went for statistical target oriented implementation of various developmental programmes like IRDP and then insistence of forest officers that the Forest Conservation Act had to be implemented both in letter and spirit created extreme degrees of unnoticed unrest amongst the tribal populace. This, in addition to the exploitation of tribals by the lower forest functionaries, was exploited by the naxalites who had started visiting Bastar as early as 1970s. The naxalites were able to gradually convince the villagers that the government was exploitive and they must fight the government. By 1980s, the naxalites had become well entrenched in southern Bastar and had started making forays in the north of the river Indrawati. In southern side of Indrawati, they had started holding Jan Adalats and beating forest officials, exploitative PHC health officials, teachers, etc., on the complaints of villager. As there was no positive interaction between the government machinery and the tribals they fell for the only people regularly interacting with them, i.e., the naxalites.

Tribal Women in Bastar

The presence of the naxalites also led to withdrawal of political functionaries from the areas frequented by naxalites, thus creating a political space for the naxalites to further entrench themselves. In a liberal democratic polity, no scheme of the government can be successful unless the people at large generally accept it. While the interaction between the government agency and the people acquire a different dynamics in non-tribal areas, in tribal areas the interactive process between the tribal and government machinery have to be extremely subtle, flexible and multi-layered.

Hut of a Tribal in Bastar

The tribal's own social hierarchal system has to be creatively utilised towards a gradual process of pragmatic education. This education has to be a two-way process in which not only the tribal is educated on the importance of the change envisaged but also the bureaucrat is educated about the tribal way of looking at things, his aspirations and his fears that should then be used to remodel the approach and strategy. This was not done leading to growing fears amongst the tribals.

Researchers with Students in a School

Obviously, the tribal society cannot remain 'frozen in time'. All societies started from tribal groups and through history encountering advanced civilisation, transformed themselves from tribal to feudal to modern societies. The change must have entailed deep traumatic encounters affecting the psyche. The tribals of Bastar also cannot be allowed to remain 'Museum pieces' in history. However, their integration with advance systems and its change to a different or higher cultural level can today be made less traumatic and debilitating for a primitive culture. Our study shows that the naxalites are equally suppressive and violent in their approach to changing the Bastar tribal as has been the Government and this should be realised by both. No interactive process is possible unless the area sees a prolonged period of peace.

Well Being Used for Drinking water and Cleaning

Pig Around Well

Tribals Taking Water from Well

Pumpkin Cover used for Storage Purpose

Ornaments of Bastar Tribes

Dry Fish in the Bastar Tribal Market

Bastar Tribal Women Selling Product in Weekly Market

I

Government—Tribal Interface in Bastar Area in the Post Independent India

The Bastar tribals, during the period when Bastar was an Independent Kingdom under British rule, virtually lived an independent and free life with very little interference from the King or the administration. The tribals were allowed to live freely in the jungle, fell trees to prepare land for cultivation, set-up new villages and generally lead a life that was not intruded upon by the outsiders. The first sign of unrest amongst the tribals of Bastar was noticed when outsiders came and settled in the area to do business, trading, etc. However, the biggest tribal unrest in Bastar took place when the first reservation of forest land was undertaken by the then princely state of Bastar in 1910 that had to be brutally suppressed by Army. When India gained Independence, lot of discussions took place amongst politicians, bureaucrats, anthropologists, sociologists and planners on how to deal with the primitive tribal societies. There were three approaches on how to deal with the primitive tribals that can be summed up as under:

(a) *Isolationist Approach:* This approach involved allowing the tribals to live in isolation and not to interfere with their life, customs, etc. It also involved not subjecting them to various developmental programmes unless there was demand for the same from the tribal groups themselves;

(b) *Integrative Approach*: This approach involved graded interaction between the tribals and the developmental/ bureaucratic agencies so that the tribal can gradually be educated and prepared for integrating with a more developed and complex cultural systems. This approach had its greatest protagonist in Pandit Jawaharlal Nehru, the first Prime Minister of India.

(c) *Assimilative Approach*: This approach believed that the tribal societies should be assimilated into the mainstream culture through positive and aggressive interventions, otherwise the gap between the primitive and the advanced and more complex societies and cultures would keep on growing. The protagonists of this approach believed that all societies were initially tribal societies and it was in their traumatic interface and struggle with advanced cultural societies that they acquired strength not only to survive but to also get assimilated and integrated into a more advanced and complex culture. In many cases, they were able themselves to transform into a parallel advanced and complex cultural system. The Indian approach in the early post-Independent period was that of gradual integration of the tribal societies into the main cultural stream in a slow, graded manner. Bastar, however, saw certain administrators who had great love and understanding of tribals. Dr B.D. Sharma, as a young Collector in Bastar conceptualised his theory of tribal development as well as worked out an elaborate framework of tribal development management. Dr Sharma questioned the theory that higher consumption means development in tribal context. He emphasised the importance of satisfying the basic needs of nourishing food for the tribal and of restoration of ecological balance in the tribal area. He argued that any super imposition of the goals of an advanced culture on tribals for higher consumption beyond the basic needs should be done with greatest caution. Sharma, however, differed from Verrier Elvin and that the tribals should be allowed to remain as they are. He wanted to adopt a middle path like Nehru and felt that the tribals should be allowed to develop along the lines of their own genius and through their own institutions and the government's interface with the tribals should be cautious, graded and gradual. He further felt that over administration and burning the tribals with a maze of economic institutions is not only uncalled for but also dangerous. He also felt that as tribal situation in India varies widely, tribal development cannot be a matter of devising a general formula for tribal development. (Today Dr B.D. Sharma has become more of an activist than a thinker and planner of tribal development and his views have been acquiring an extremist tinge.) However, in practice, it was given ago-by and the Govt. tried to impose its will through various programmes that were not acceptable to the tribal, leading to various kinds of apprehensions and fears in his mind. The educational system imposed on him was different from the one he was familiar with in the tribal society.

The Government's institutions and the success of the governmental programmes depend on two things:

1. Good governance, and
2. Adoption of the programmes by the people. This can be shown as under: This includes, the government people social interaction, good governance and adoption of programmes by the people. It would be clear that this would also depend on the nature and intensity of the social interaction between a government, which has to be benignly persuasive and educative and the people. It has to be underpinned by good governance because bad and oppressive governance would generate fear that would obstruct social interaction.

This can be shown as under:

- The government people
- Social interaction
- Good governance
- Adoption of programme by the people

Here, the break in the social interactions would indicate that people would not easily accept and adopt the programmes of the government. Similarly, if the governance was bad or poor, the social interaction would again break, leading to the same negative result. If this happens, then the people would open up to different ideologies, philosophies or strategies or decide to become more isolationists. It is also important that the interface between the government and the people is done in such a graded manner that at all levels the objectives of the government coincide with the larger objectives and goals of the people. This can be shown as under: That this kind of social interaction between the government and the tribals of Bastar did not exist is obvious from the fact that the tribals moved towards a different ideology. It must be understood that the tribal of Bastar has refused to accept that the forest no more belongs to them. They have lived in the forest for centuries. An educated tribal told the team—we tribals have lived in jungles for centuries; we depend on it; we know how to take care of it. Whenever do illegal felling. The forests are being denuded by commercial felling of trees by the Forest Department and illegal felling by contractors. If the Objective of the Chhatisgarh Implementation of the vision of the Govt., the programmes Distric Block Panchayat tribals were allowed to have their traditional rights on forest, only if it is absolutely required for survival. Further as tribals' religion is a primitive one, many of the trees are treated as Gods and cannot be cut." Had the government taken the tribals in confidence and made them partners in forest management, the tribal would not have felt that they have been deprived of some thing, which belongs to them for centuries.

In addition, the land hunger of Bastar tribals is increasing everyday. As most of the land is a reserved forest, land holdings are progressively becoming smaller and uneconomical. Earlier, if land grew scarce, a group would leave the village, clear some forest and form a new village. The new forest policy deprived the tribals of this freedom. Further, large areas of forest also being converted for wild life sanctuary under Project Tiger also necessitated uprooting of tribals villages from those areas. The attachment of tribals with the village Gods, trees, totems are not 'archetypical' but very real and the forest policy affected the tribals' psyche in a serious and adverse manner. Similarly, in the early 80s proposal to construct World Bank financed Bodhghat Dam on the Indrawati river as well a project of Forest Department to replace large areas of Sal Forest with tropical pine trees had led to a fair degree of tribal unrest leading to a movement which forced the government to abandon both the programmes. If the affected Bastar tribals were taken in confidence before a decision was taken to dam Indrawati or replace sal forest with tropical pines, the government could have avoided confrontation and subsequent loss of crores of rupees, which was spent before both the projects were scrapped. The tribals of Bastar have also lost faith in the judiciary system, which has been imposed on them. The tribal concept of justice is delivering 'instant' judgement through a democratic process of discussion in tribal panchayat normally taken unanimously. Further, the tribal traditions of punishment are normally merciful and lenient and the defaulter is normally fined and made to organise a feast for the villagers. He does not accept the Indian judicial system because of the inherent delays in the system, his forced frequent presence in the courts and his feelings that more often than not the defaulter escapes punishment. In jail he suffers in acute and subtle ways. His ordinary life is so free, his needs so few and simple, his life depends so entirely on certain stimulants like his trees, his liquor, his dances, his songs that without them he quickly loses desire to live in a prison. After his release, he returns to his village, a diseased and a sick person. The above geographical and socio-economic reality of Bastar must be properly understood if the reasons for the growth of naxalism in Bastar are to be understood. Tribals of Bastar inhabit the thick Sal and Teak forests that also happen to be rich in industrial minerals such as iron ore, dolomite, limestone, corundum (Ruby), tin and uranium. These areas were subjected to commercial exploitation for timber as well as for minerals to feed industries not situated there. Because of the above, the rights enjoyed by the tribals in the forest were drastically curtailed. The mining areas of NMDC not only dispossessed them of their land but also forced many women amongst them to a life of prostitution. On the other hand, the Forest Conservation Act drastically reduced the rights they had enjoyed in the forest. Not properly educated in the necessity of mineral exploitation, not properly compensated for their rights curtailed, the tribal of Bastar started viewing the State and the government as a permanent threat to his life, economy and culture. The reality of the tribal in Bastar is largely dependent on the forest for his daily living. Firewood, timber and thatch for housing, fodder for cattle, edible roots, herbs, fish and occasional animals for hunting, tie him both economically and emotionally to the forest. Agriculture has been traditionally only a supplement and not the mainstay of the economy of the Bastar tribal.

With the coming of the Forest Conservation Act, no fresh forest could be cleared by tribals to increase the food production. This placed a tremendous pressure on available land. Further, the exploitative forest officials especially at the lower rungs also deprived him of minor forest produce to which he was entitled legally but was unaware. Scientific forest management for 'national interest' also deprived his cattle's grazing space. Instead of compassionate interaction between the state machinery and the tribal, he was to witness harassment and frequent violence by the lower functionaries of the forest department. The additional problem that the tribal was facing was the plunder of forest produce by outsider merchants with government standing aloof as silent spectator and the mainstream politicians as well as the bureaucrats openly supporting the merchants for obvious reasons. Another major contributor towards the unease of Bastar tribals was unimaginative implementation of various developmental programmes. While the objectives of many of these programmes were laudable, some amount of adaptation was called for in addition to proper education of the tribal. In the absence of the above, the tribal felt extremely apprehensive. The tyranny of a target-based programme also creates all kinds of social dysfunctions in the area where such programmes are implemented. It was the aforementioned situation that existed in Bastar area when the naxalites started moving in from Andhra Pradesh.

II

Naxalism and its Growth in Bastar

The Maoists, who believe in the principle of armed struggle for bringing about a revolution and dismantling what they term as 'bourgeois capitalist democracy', have always formed a determined group amongst the Indian Communists. Earlier, they were part of the Communist Party of India but when the CPI started following an exclusively pro-Russian line, the pro-Maoists broke away to form the CPI(Marxist). When the CPI(Marxist) also decided to take part in Parliamentary and Assembly elections, those who considered themselves as purists broke away to form the Coordinating Committee of Communist Revolutionaries under the leadership of Charu Majumdar, who felt that India was ripe for an armed revolution, and started his movement in Naxalbari believing in the Maoist dictum that 'a spark would cause a prairie fire'. However, when the armed struggle actually started, sharp differences arose amongst the Maoists and the movement got divided into various factions, which developed different strategies and tactics for taking the movement forward. Bastar borders the naxalite-infested districts of Andhra Pradesh and between 1948 and 1952 it was used as a peaceful 'terra incognita' for the communist revolutionaries of Khammam, Warangal, Karimnagar and Adilabad districts. The area of south Bastar was well known to the Maoists. According to senior journalists working in Bastar, the naxalites from Andhra Pradesh started visiting southern Bastar from 1968 to propagate their ideologies as well as to use the area as a shelter. Initially, their movement in southern Bastar went unnoticed but after 1980 when their movements in southern Bastar dramatically increased, the state government of Madhya Pradesh became alert. According to a very senior journalist, the naxalite group that frequented southern Bastar before 1980 were C. P. Reddy's group, pro-Lin Biao group and sometimes, Rauf's group. After 1980, it was Kondapalli Seetharamaiah's People's War Group, which became active in southern Bastar. The groups belonging to C. P. Reddy, Rauf and pro-Lin Biao faction soon lost whatever little hold they had in southern Bastar. After 1980, the naxalites started moving freely in the police station areas of Konta, Golapalli, Usoor, Tarlaguda and Bhopal patnam. They were soon able to push their activities in certain areas of Bijapur, Jagargunda and Sukma police station areas. The naxalites soon started influencing the tribals by speaking against the excesses committed by contactors and forest, revenue and police officials. They openly held meetings in tribal villages and opposed the removal of tribal villages from reserve forest land. They soon started pressurising the contractors to increase wages of labour substantially. In short, the naxalites started taking up any cause that was intimately connected with the life of the tribal. They soon started holding *Jan Adalats* and started punishing petty forest officials working in the area for their alleged corruption or misbehaviour. The above as well as the linguistic affinity between the members of the naxalite *dalams* and the Telugu speaking Dorla tribals started winning the naxalites a sizeable number of sympathisers and well-wishers.

According to a senior Bastar journalist, by 1982-83, the naxalites were freely moving in about 1200 sq. km south of Indrawati River. This journalist, who had followed the naxalite movement and was present in one of the *Jan Adalats,* stated that the naxalite *dalam,* usually entered a village after sunset and talked to the tribal chief of the village so that a meeting of the villagers could be organised. At the meeting, the naxalite leader would enquire about atrocities committed on them by Government officials, whether the teacher was taking the classes in the school regularly, whether the doctor was present in the

Primary Health Centres on all days, whether the tribal was being paid regularly and properly by the forest officials for working in the forest, etc. The villagers were told that the forest was their inheritance and they were free to encroach upon the forestland for cultivation. In case of complaints against petty forest and revenue officers, these officers were caught and brought to the *Jan Adalats* and either threatened or beaten. Some *dalam* members would then distribute free medicines among the tribals for minor ailments. The meeting would normally end with some revolutionary song and all the tribals attending the meeting would join the naxalites in singing these. As songs were invariably in Telugu, it was not difficult for the Dorla tribals to understand it. A free English translation of one of such songs was available with the journalist that is given below:

"O Revenue Patwari
O Police Inspector
O Forest Ranger
O Khakhi clad fools and 'Chamchas' of Congress

The Adivasis have woken from their slumbers and are out for your blood,

You have been fattened by eating free chicken of the villagers. Have drunk their liquor free. The Advasis are after your blood. O You fat-bellied fools. Wearing good clothes and riding motor cycles. Friends of rich villagers. The Adivasis will remove your toe-nails. Shave your head, moustaches, eye brows. Remove your clothes and Branch your tummies with hot iron. Beware, fools the Adivasis have awakened they will cut your throats."

The psychological impact, which such songs repeated again and again, would have on the minds of tribals, could be imagined. While theoretical indoctrination of the Bastar tribal was never done, 'emotional indoctrination' started around 1980. For the first 10-12 years, the naxalites' treatment of the tribals was reasonably good and they would try to keep the tribal village Chiefs and the Witch Doctors (Sirhas) in good humour. After around the 90s, they started becoming more violent, oppressive and intolerant. Soon the naxalites were no more polite with the tribal village chiefs and they would frequently be beaten up or even killed if they had differences of opinion with the naxalite dalam leaders. The naxalites showed a fair degree of intolerance towards tribal superstition, their religions and their customs. There were also cases of naxalites insulting the tribal totems. They seemed to be in a hurry to create an intellectual-psychological atmosphere to impart theoretical aspects of their ideology. This led to a fair degree of psychological stress and unrest amongst the tribals but this was ruthlessly crushed by the naxalites because of their superior armed power. This was also the period that the naxalites started collecting 'rent' from contractors, both civil and forest, as well as 'Tendu leaf' contractors, government officials etc. While the tribal may not have an understanding of monetary affairs to enable him to realise its implication in totality, at the same time, he is not a fool to understand that the money collected by the naxalites in his name was not really being utilised for his benefit and this further increased his sense of unease.

Obviously, the naxalites had landed themselves in a peculiar situation. As a political party (and this is true for all political parties), it needed money for maintaining its various infrastructures, publicity organs, publication of magazines, pamphlets etc. As an underground political movement that depended on armed struggle as its main weapon, it needed more money for purchase of arms and ammunitions and explosives as well as to develop facilities to maintain these. As an underground armed movement it also needed money for the treatment of its underground cadres, fight cases to ensure release of cadres arrested, etc. Thus, they not only needed large sums of money, they could not spend much of it on development of the tribals for whom they were allegedly fighting their battle with the 'bourgeois capitalist government'.

The tribal is a very simple and uncomplicated person and thus he also has very clear eyes. He could not understand the necessity of large money collections. He could also see that most of this was not being utilised for his good. In its urge to expand fast and control the area in accordance with its own ideology and agenda, the naxalites started making the same mistake that the government had made earlier. Both the naxalites and the government started acting in an elitist fashion that basically is an assertion that only they know what is correct and true and the others are ignoramuses. However, in spite of some unease and unrest among the tribals about the naxalites, more and more naxalite cadres were pushed into Bastar area and soon the naxalites held sway in the whole of Bijapur and Dantewada area and even crossed river Indrawati and captured the whole of the Abhuj Mad area. According to local people, the naxalites have been able to establish some control in certain pockets of Narainpur, Kondagaon, Bhanupratappur, Keskal police station areas.

III

Salwa Judum Movement—Response of Government, Political Leaders and Naxalites

In June 2005, the tribals of 25-26 villages in Bijapur police district held anti-naxalite rally at Mathwada Weekly Market in PS Jangla area. According to people of the area, this rally did not have any leader. The immediate provocation for this kind of rally is stated to be seen as unemployment of the tribals. It appears that the Tendu Leaf contractors and the naxalites could not come to an agreement. The naxalites were demanding much higher 'rent' as well as forcing the Tendu Leaf contractors to give higher wages to the tribals also. As a result, the Tendu Leaf contractors decided not to submit tenders for picking Tendu Leaf in the area. Seasonal picking up of Tendu Leaf has provided seasonal employment to the tribals for ages. As the agricultural productivity in the area is low, the tribals cannot totally depend on agriculture and has to take course to seasonal employment to augment his economy. With the contractors withdrawing from the area, the tribals financial situation became precarious leading to the rally. This was not the first time that such unrest was noticed in the area. According to the knowledgeable people in Bastar, a similar anti-naxalite tribal unrest was witnessed in the latter part of 1990 but was brutally subdued and suppressed by the naxalites.

The tribals called their movement Salva Judum. In the Maria dialect, 'Salva' means sprinkling of holy water over a sick person with a wish to make him healthy. 'Judum' means the community. Thus, Salva Judum basically means to sprinkle holy water over the community, which has been inflicted by the 'disease of naxalism'. Somehow, the word has been misinterpreted to mean 'peace march'. This term would show how much the tribal was incensed to call the naxalite intervention 'a disease'. Obviously, the withdrawal of Tendu Leaf contractors from the area, which deprived the tribals of seasonal employment, could not be the only reason as the tribal could have still subsisted on other kinds of minor forest produce, including edible roots, etc. The reasons have to go deeper. Our survey in the villages indicated that the undercurrent of tribal unrest against the naxalites existed for quite some time mainly because the latter's treatment of the tribals and their total disregard for tribal customs and religion, including their totems and village Gods. There is an allegation by the naxalites, some civil liberty bodies and articles written by journalists that Salva Judum movement is sponsored by the Chhattisgarh Government. Even the Independent Citizens Initiative has called it a 'state sponsored' movement. However, a movement which is involving 40000-45000 people cannot be sponsored by a government which could not put its acts together to even plan, formalise and implement its own developmental strategies in the area in the past and gave the opportunity to the naxalite to enter and get entrenched. It is too much to expect that the same government conceived, planned and implemented such a movement and could do so using the police or its lower revenue and forest functionaries. Even if it is accepted that the movement started spontaneously and was later hijacked by the government and politicians, it is difficult to accept that it could be sustained for such a long duration unless people involved have deep grudge and animosity towards the naxalites. At least five different teams have confirmed that nearly 46000 people are living in the camps, which have appalling living conditions. Some of them are now settled by the roadside and there are plans to establish over 500 new villages. It is also learnt that the government has appointed around 3500 Special Police Officers who are being paid Rs 1500 p.m. with a promise of getting a regular employment in the police force at a future date. People who intimately know the tribals of Bastar would realise that the Bastar tribal's economic needs are minimal. He puts much greater value on his freedom. He loves his jungles, his trees, especially the Sago Palm Tree (Sulfie) which he or his forefathers have planted, his village Gods and Totems, etc., too intimately and intensely to forego these to come and live in a congested relief camp unless there are very compelling reasons to go so. If one sees a Bastar tribal village, one would realise that it is not like villages in other parts of the country. The villages are spread out in large areas with cluster of four to five houses at one place followed by open space and then again similar clusters of four to five houses in various directions. The reaction to the first Salva Judum rally at Mathwada Weekly Market in Bijapur area on 18th June, 2005 saw a quick retaliation by the naxalites who killed three tribals who had attended that rally. This led to the first migration of 3000 tribal villagers to Bijapur and another thousand to Named.

However, undeterred by the killings, the tribals of Bhairamgarh area took out another anti-naxalite rally on June 22, 2005 followed by yet another rally on June 25 at Nalgoda in Dantewada area, where the tribals decided to form Village Defence Committees. On the very same day, another similar rally was organised in Bijapur, which was the first rally to be addressed by a Congress MLA, local politicians and Panchayat leaders. The next day, June 26th, another rally was organised at Named in Bijapur area, which was addressed for the first time by Mahendra Karma, Congress MLA from Dantewada. It was here that the first indications of Mahendra Karma attempting to take over the leadership of Salva Judum movement were evident.

According to knowledgeable people of Bastar, Mahendra Karma, who was earlier a CPI MLA from Dantewada, was never happy with the growth of the naxalite influence in Bastar. It is said that even in the early 80s, as services of tribal students who owed their allegiance to AISF. That he was not able to contain the naxalite growth in the area was also due to the fact that at that time his influence was limited to certain areas of Dantewada. Apart from his ideological differences with naxalite brand of communism, he could not muster the support of other politicians and the government of the day. Karma later joined the Congress party and saw in the Salva Judum movement an opportunity to emerge as an undisputed Maria leader. Since, many in the Congress were apprehensive that Mahendra Karma may acquire a more important status in the party; the first opposition to Karma also came from certain leaders within the Congress. There was another reason for this opposition. A democratic polity depends on elections. In geographical areas, which are affected by insurgency and underground extremists movement, the leaders of various political parties still have to fight elections. To ensure that elections are not unduly disturbed, they mostly develop a back channel or underground linkage with extremists or insurgent leaders. A movement that may lead to open confrontation between groups of people is likely to make their position extremely untenable and hence there is a tendency to demand a peaceful *status quo* not as a Gandhian strategy of political action but to ensure safe electoral politics.

As the naxalite attacks on Salva Judum supporters continued and intensified (according to reports, more than 200 Salva Judum supporters have been killed so far), tribals started migrating to safer areas close to police stations. It is here that the State Government accepted its responsibility to provide security and established relief camps. According to journalists working in Bastar and Raipur, the State Government saw in the movement an opportunity not only to attack the naxalite ideology but also to debunk the naxalites' claim that they are working for the betterment of the tribals. As the naxalites started attacking the relief camps, security forces had to be augmented in the area and today, the entire area of Bastar is full of CRPF and other security forces either protecting the relief camps or going out on combing and anti-naxalite operations. The Government's support to Salva Judum interestingly brought Mahendra Karma, a Congress MLA and Dr Raman Singh, the BJP Chief Minister, who should have been natural political adversaries, close. Glancing through the anti-Salva Judum literatures that are being constantly posted on pro-Left websites, one gets the impression that the Salva Judum movement has taken the naxalites by surprise. There is talk of violence being perpetrated by Salva Judum supporters on hapless tribals. The Salva Judum movement has been constantly declared as government-sponsored and it is being alleged that it, with the support of security forces, was burning down villages, raping women, killing tribals and forcing villagers to come to Salva Judum camps. While it is true that during the field studies the team were able to verify some cases of atrocities committed by Salva Judum supporters in the initial period of the movement and huts of tribals who were supporting the naxalites were burnt down and that a fair degree of violence was perpetrated, such incidents have drastically come down. This can be attributed to the psychological make-up of the Bastar tribal whose emotional threshold is low. In fact, the entire area of the undivided district of Bastar even otherwise witnesses a very large number of murders and suicides. There are some inputs to indicate security forces that came from other states (especially the Nagaland Armed Police) were ruthless in its operations. It is also possible that the state police, which was so far at the receiving end in Bastar, gave vent to its anger during anti-naxalite operations as they were now being helped by some Salva Judum supporters and surrendered Sangham members (earlier naxalites). The allegation of molestation and rape by Salva Judum supporters has to be taken with a pinch of salt because the Bastar tribal is generally not known for indulging in molestation and rape. The allegation by pro-Left websites as well as some study groups that has visited Bastar for a short duration regarding how they found police officers drunk and Salva Judum supporters actually running the show, terrorising people blocking roads, etc., are observations that need some discussion. One thing, which the team could observe during its visits to different parts of Bastar, was that the local police station staffs look normally unkempt and possibly even drunk. The tribal of Bastar, whether living in Salva Judum relief camps or in the villages, also loves his *Taddy* and *Mahua* liquor and as a result of its consumption, usually becomes boisterous. Even before the naxalites came to Bastar, any one who has lived in Bastar for many years would attest to the facts that it was not uncommon for tribals blockading roads for collecting money after they became boisterous due to intake of Mahua liquor. It was also customary for people using the road to pay them a small token amount after which they would be allowed to proceed. It is also common knowledge that during Dussehra festival and Rath festival in Bastar, there is a custom of tribals stealing the Rath and taking it to a forest close to the town from where they are cajoled to bring back the Rath and while they are bringing back the Rath to the town, the boisterous Maria tribal youth would indulge in looting small items from various shops falling on the wayside. Any study team that is not aware of the tribal mores, customs, traditions, their worldview and their psychological make-up and visits Bastar only for a few days is likely to misinterpret the tribal behaviour according to his own belief system. This is not to say that Salva Judum supporters themselves or under connivance or actual instigation from police did not indulge in violence here and there.

What we are trying to suggest is that the reports which are being posted by pro-Left website and various study teams appear to be highly exaggerated. What seems to be true is that the Salva Judum movement was a spontaneous uprising against actual or perceived grievances of the tribals in Bijapur area against the naxalites. When the naxalites retaliated against the Salva Judum supporters with violence instead of engaging them in a discussion to find out about their grievances, the movement picked up. Subsequently, Mahendra Karma, a Maria himself and a Congress MLA and leader of the opposition, jumped in and took over the leadership for his own political designs. With the naxalite violence against Salva Judum supporters being further stepped up, the tribals were forced to move for safer places which led to the establishment of relief camps by the Government. Dr Raman Singh, Chief Minister of Chhatisgarh, who was finding it difficult to implement the developmental strategies of his government in Bastar or to checkmate and push back the influence of naxalites from the area because of a visionless, corrupt and lethargic bureaucracy, and an inefficient, untrained and corrupt police force, found in Salva Judum a movement which could be used to weaken the naxalite influence in the area. This is the reason why he must have decided to back Mahendra Karma, otherwise his political adversary. Whether the Salva Judum movement can sustain itself cannot be predicted with any degree of certainty. It would depend on various factors. The natural tendency of a Bastar tribal is not to live in a congested environment. There are reports about corruption because of large amount of funds pouring in from State and the Centre for various relief schemes and the Salva Judum supporters are also aware of it. However, as long as the naxalite violence against the Salva Judum supporters living in camps or villages continues, the tribal would be afraid to leave the camp and go back to his village. Thus, the continued naxalite violence is guaranteeing the continuation of relief camps. On the other hand, the corruption of officials involved in relief work may finally incense the Salva Judum supporters and force them to buy peace with the naxalites and go back to their villages. After all, there is very little to choose between the violence of one and corrupt immorality of the other.

IV

Findings and Observations of the Study Team which Visited the Bastar Area between (December 2006–January 2007)

Bastar and its problems cannot be understood on short visits. On the other hand, outsiders who settled in Bastar for trading, business and farming have also developed vested interests and tend to twist perspective. Those who settled down in Bastar since the days when Bastar was a princely kingdom came from various states. There are Maithili Brahmins from Darbhanga, Bihar who came to Bastar because the Raj Purohit of Bastar State was a Maithili Brahmin and many Maithils, either related to the Raj Purohit's family or close to his family came and settled down in Bastar. Many of them started working as officials in the Bastar State and some were given tracts of land for cultivation. Others came from parts of Bihar, UP and Rajasthan and started working as forest contractors and traders. As the original Bastar Kings belonged to the Kakatiya Dynasty of Warangal, many people also came and settled from Andhra Pradesh. As the Kings of Bastar also developed matrimonial linkages with the Mayurbhanj Dynasty in Orissa, a large number of Oriya population also settled down in Bastar.

In addition to the above, various people from other parts of Chhatisgarh have settled in Bastar. Most of them have a very low opinion about the aboriginals who are the original inhabitants of Bastar. They generally feel that naxalites are goons and dacoits who should be ruthlessly suppressed. They have very little anthropological and sociological understanding of the tribals. The study team decided not to utilise the material they gathered from these outside settlers. The study team met Mahendra Karma and his supporters but found any fruitful discussion with them difficult.

One cannot blame Karma. He has projected himself as a leader of Salva Judum movement and has very fixed views about his importance and his role in the movement. After interacting with Karma, the study team decided not to interact with mainstream politicians and bureaucrats because it felt that their responses would be according to party lines or stock bureaucratic responses. The team visited 20 tribal villages and six Haats where tribals of various villages congregate for making purchases of essential items and selling their own produce. While interacting with the tribals, the team members realised that it was difficult to make them respond to a question answer format and decided to introduce a more congenial interview/discussion format. The study team also realised that leading questions do not get a true response. It was realised that while the tribal's psychological threshold is low and he can be provoked into anger.

Occasionally, he is normally in a non-combative mood and may decide to agree with you and say 'yes' to your leading questions. Thus, the methodology used was to draw the tribal into a general discussion and gradually insert questions about the naxalite movement, Salva Judum and the government's developmental schemes in an indirect manner. Once the tribal opens up, he normally gives an anthropologist, a wealth of information. The Bastar tribal also has a simple but a queer sense of humour. The survey team during its visit to villages and haats in southern Bastar talked to nearly 100 people which included around 23 naxalites/Sangham members and villagers who supported the naxalites, 25 Salva Judum supporters and around 52 tribals who neither supported the government and Salva Judum movement nor the naxalites.

The findings of the study team, during interaction with non-committed tribal villagers of southern Bastar are given as under:

1. Most of them felt that the government's policy, especially the forest policy has brought uncalled for the tribals. There was a general feeling that the forest officials had exploited the tribals. Some of them complained of forest officers' usual threat of dispossessing them of land in forest villages as well as non-payment for labour done in their houses, non-payment for chicken and liquor taken away by forest guards and rangers, etc. There were similar complaints against police station staff and other government employees. Nearly, all villagers stated that doctors were mostly unavailable at Primary Health Centres.
2. The tribals were also critical of various developmental programmes, which included constructions of roads and bridges because of ill treatment by engineers and contractors. They also complained that most of the engineers and government employees had no understanding of the sentiments they attach to their totems and villages Gods and would often uproot the totems and throw them aside while constructing the roads. When asked whether the villagers do not want their villages to be connected with roads and facilitate communication and easy movement, most of the tribals stated that they would like roads and bridges to be constructed but they do not want their totems and village Gods to be insulted in the process.
3. Most of the villagers also stated that when the naxalites came to Bastar, they were voicing their concerns and their presence forced the forest and other officials to start behaving properly. This made the naxalites very popular. However, the naxalites soon started behaving in an oppressive and intrusive manner, which brought about an emotional breakdown between the naxalites and the tribals. When asked whether the tribals showed their anger at this, the tribals stated that the naxalites were armed and would ruthlessly suppress any opposition. The tribals also stated that the naxalites had also started belittling their Gods. In fact, they often called all their beliefs stupid.
4. When they were told that the study team has also talked to some tribals who supported the naxalites, the villagers

stated that it was true that most villagers are now divided into pro-naxalite and anti-naxalite groups. The pro-naxalite groups normally consist of those tribals who have the support of naxalites and feel empowered. They, however, stated that most of the villagers do not support the naxalites but have to remain silent fearing naxalite reprisal.

5. On whether they support Salva Judum movement, many tribals stated that they support the movement as it would finally bring some sense in the naxalites, but many tribals refused to comment or take side because they were not sure whether government would really look after them. On the other hand, interactions with Salva Judum supporters showed that the tribals have fair degree of anger against the naxalites.

The information and reactions of the tribals, which could be gathered, are given below:

1. The Salva Judum supporters castigated the naxalites as immoral people who are only interested in collecting money from contractors, traders and such people who had been exploiting the tribals for ages.
2. They further stated that while the naxalites claim to be working for the betterment of tribals in Bastar, they take money and befriend only rich people who pay them money. One educated tribal youth from Bacheli stated that while the NMDC project is targeted by then Naxalites, the ESSAR Project which only a few kilometres away from NMDC project is never attacked because the ESSAR people have agreed to pay huge amount of money for their protection. He also stated that the facilities of private contractors working in NMDC are never attacked because the contractors also pay them 'protection money'.
3. Another Salva Judum supporter stated that while the naxalites collect so much money and claim that they would use it for the betterment of tribals, in reality, hardly any money is spent for the development of the tribals. When the Salva Judum supporters were asked that, according to some reports, the naxalites have been running mobile schools and Chaitanya Natya Manch and Mandalis for

cultural and informal education, the supporters stated that one must count how many such mobile schools are being run by the naxalites. When the Salva Judum supporters were asked about certain reports in magazines and journals about naxalites also involving themselves in developmental work like digging of wells and ponds and other minor irrigation work, the tribals again stated that the team should find out how many such activities have been undertaken by the naxalites. Another Salva Judum supporter stated that the naxalites have done some developmental work but the labour was actually done by villagers for which the naxalites made no payments insisting that it was Shramdan for a new society. He said that how is this different from 'begar' they were forced to do for the rich and the government and forest officials working in the area.

4. Many Salva Judum supporters also stated that naxalites are destroying their culture. They stated that the naxalites have no understanding or love for their social customs, religion and values and are persuading tribals to leave these for their way of life.
5. When questioned about whether they support the government, many kept quiet but some stated that they are happy that the government is giving them security without which they would have found difficult to fight the naxalites as naxalites know no mercy. When questioned deeply whether they support various government policies, some of the tribals stated that as long as the government's policy are designed to develop the area without trying to hurt their sentiments or becoming exploitative, they would support the government's developmental programmes. Some Salva Judum supporters, however, stated that if the government becomes 'bad' then it would also face a Salva Judum movement against itself.
6. Probing about the conditions of relief camps most of the Salva Judum supporters stated that they do not want to live in the camps forever and would like to go back to their villages as soon as the naxalites are pushed out of the area. They love their village, their forest, their Gods too much to

leave too much to permanently settle down in or around relief camps.

7. When Salva Judum supporters were told that there are reports that they are indulging in violence against those tribals who do not agree with Salva Judum movement, the tribals stated that some violence has been committed but it was only against those people who along with naxalites perpetuated violence against them when they were weak and divided. They totally denied the allegations that they have indulged in looting, etc., because some of them have been made Special Police Officers and have been given guns. Some of them said that sometimes youths after drinking may have stopped passersby for money after they exhausted their own money for more liquor but this the tribal youths used to do even when Salva Judum movement had not begun and they fail to understand what is wrong in asking for money from someone who has if they need it but have exhausted their own money. Some Salva Judum supporters, however, accepted that they have assisted the police in road checking but stated that it was policeman who was taking money from buses and taxis and not the Salva Judum supporters.
8. When they were questioned about allegations that the Salva Judum movement is being led by non-tribals, most of them stated that the non-tribals in the movement are not leaders but only friends of Mahendra Karma or those with whom the tribals had interacted for along time. The team members were also able to meet naxalite supporters and active naxalite cadres during the field study. Most of the naxalites talked of the importance of class struggle and highlighted the fact that the naxalite movement and the Salva Judum movement have to be seen as a normal accentuation in the class struggle. They asserted that Salva Judum movement was sponsored by a reactionary capitalist government, which has used its huge resources to befool simple tribals into fighting with their own brothers. The naxalites were sure that the government as well as Salva Judum supporters would finally be defeated. They stated that the naxalites know that the battle against immoral

capitalist government would take a long time but were certain that the final victory would be theirs as no government can for long take on the people's revolution. When the naxalites were told that this long battle which they are talking about would keep the whole country in turmoil and that no development even for the exploited masses for whom they are fighting this war can be achieved unless the atmosphere of peace is maintained for a long duration, the naxalites stated that development on proper lines would start only after they demolish the present corrupt political structure and replace it by a system based on tenets of Maoism.

They further stated that the masses which have remained poor and exploited for such a long time can definitely sacrifice a 'bad' today for a much better 'tomorrow'. When questioned about how they feel about killings of innocent people in the name of suppressing Salva Judum movement, the naxalites said that they are fighting a war and in all wars some innocent people unfortunately get killed. While they are sad that innocents get killed as long as the war continues, such unfortunate killings would continue to take place. They further defended mass killings of policemen by using explosives and landmines on the plea that in all wars those who support the adversaries have to be treated as enemies and killed. It may be mentioned here that during interactions with naxalites it was one person who would interact with the team, the rest would just nod their heads in agreement.

Some of the other important interactions with the naxalites in southern Bastar are summarised below:

1. When they were asked that while they allege that the state has done nothing for the tribals what have they done for the tribals in the last 25-30 years, have been in Dandakaranya area, the naxalites stated that they have made their life less exploitative. They have done many things to improve the lot of the tribals. But most importantly they have given them a vision of what a non-exploitative culture should be and that it is attainable through class struggle.

2. When they were asked that while they talk of a non-exploitative and amoral world they have themselves been taking money from corrupt government officials and capitalist contractors and traders, the naxalites flatly refused to accept the allegation. They stated that while money is being collected, most of it is collected through donations. They agreed that fines are levied on class enemies but according to them this forms a very small part of their collected funds. They stated that as a political party, which is involved in an armed struggle with a corrupt capitalist government, they need funds for running their various programmes, publicity, procurement of arms etc.
3. When pointed out that while they criticise and debunk the so called corrupt capitalist system, they are ready to utilise its legal system to get bail or get acquitted when arrested and charge-sheeted, the naxalites stated that they have no respect for the Indian Constitution or its laws. But as they are fighting a war, they would, as tactics, always utilise its weaknesses to strengthen their movement and they find nothing wrong in it. In all wars the weakness of the enemy is exploited. They do not agree with Gandhi's method of accepting that they have committed an offence under law but take a moral stand that they are correct in doing so and are prepared to be punished. They added that if they were not successful in utilising the weaknesses of the legal system, they would resort to operations like Jehanabad jail break to free their cadres and supporters. They also stated that they find nothing wrong in looting police weapons or forcing traders, businessmen and government officials to give donations to their party because they actually have no right over their weapons or money earned through corruption and exploitation.
4. When pointed out that the Communist movement has failed worldwide and even in Mao's China it has been replaced by a kind of a Military-Elite dictatorship to facilitate China to go on a fast track capitalist developmental model and that even in Nepal, the CPN(Maoist) had to finally agree to broker peace and become part of a democratic government, the naxalites stated that all those who have diverted from

the path laid down by Mao will finally suffer. They were extremely critical of Prachanda and Bhattarai of CPN(Maoist) for betraying the revolution. While most of the naxalites, during the interactions, came out with the aforementioned arguments, there was one naxalite leader who met the team and stated that he personally agrees that peace negotiation with the government is the best alternative as the naxalites-state confrontation has reached some kind of a stalemate situation. He stated that while there has been a lot of killings and casualties on both sides, the movement is not inching forward. He, however, stated that his party, the CPI(Maoist) has like other parties a hierarchal order and those at the helm of affairs do not believe that peace negotiation should be conducted at this time as these leaders feel that their hold would continue to grow gradually and engulf the whole country in years to come. He stated that he personally believes and there are many in his party who agree with him, that the time is ripe to not only start peace talks with the government but to enter electoral politics to strengthen the Leftist forces. He also felt that entering electoral politics would also give the party a realistic picture about its own mass support base.

This naxalite leader seemed to be reasonably educated and fluent and the team had a feeling that he was also reasonably senior in rank as he was guarded by three to four armed men in Olive green military type uniform. The naxalite refused to disclose his name stating that even he gives his name it would be a wrong name. The interactions of the study team with the naxalite revealed that while there may be some naxalites belonging to CPI(Maoist) group operating in Bastar who feel that their party should go in for peace negotiations, the official line of the party is to continue with their brand of armed class struggle. It was also evident that they are not greatly concerned about developments of tribals in the area in near future because of their holding on to their belief and conviction that the Indian democratic system, the Indian laws and the Indian Constitution can be totally dismantled after a prolonged armed struggle which they would win. The naxalites also openly indicated that they have no compunction in utilising the 'weaknesses' in Indian Constitution, legal systems and administrative procedure nor do they have any hesitancy in using in other institutions of a democratic system to further their objectives.

Conclusion

We had in the preface stated that the study team members had different political inclinations and therefore a decision was taken to keep our individual ideologies, political leaning and inclinations in abeyance to keep our empirical study free from contamination. The study, so far, has been based on what we saw and heard during our field tours. However, in the concluding part of the study we are compelled to raise certain issues, which have ideological and political implications. We believe that as long as there is violence and turbulence in Bastar the final sufferer would be the tribal of Bastar.

However, his major problem today is that apart from belonging to a very primitive tribal culture, he has been traumatised by developments in more manners than one. He is also today sandwiched between two very different competing ideologies. On one side is the bourgeois capitalists-socialists democratic system based on a written Constitution, written laws and procedures, institutions, etc. One can call this ideology a liberal socialist democracy. While this democracy is not considered to be an ideal system by many political thinkers, there is also a near unanimity that this system gives space for competitive ideologies to function in a peaceful manner. On the other hand, there is an ideology, which totally debunks the liberal-democratic system. This ideology believes in using an armed revolution to totally destroy and replace it with its own belief system and structure. The Constitutionalists would have us believe that the Constitution is sacrosanct and it cannot undergo any change. They would go to the extent to say that India, its people, its institutions, its laws are all 'creatures of the Constitution', which means, we are what we are because our Constitution says so. On the other hand, there is a historical interpretation which states that Constitutions change because history changes. History is never stagnant. It continues to develop and throws up new challenges, which were never thought of when the Constitution was written. In fact, history also forces ideologies to undergo changes. It throws up new ideologies when the old one shows rigidity to any change and replaces it. Mostly, however, one sees adjustments taking place. However, if one of the ideologies refuses to make any adjustment because of its revolutionary fervour then there would only be strife till one of the ideologies gets defeated and displaced. The people who, however, suffer in this clash are the common people who are more interested in their day-to-day existence as are being witnessed in Bastar. The historical problem of a 'nondemocratic' ideology (as even the Communists of all shades like this word 'democracy' and have reinterpreted for their own use) is that it seldom gives opportunity to a competitive ideology to even survive. In its belief that it is the only correct system, it tends to become elitist and oppressive. For after all who will decide but its leaders what is correct? This brings in wake great repressions as were witnessed in both USSR and China. Non criticism of leaders and their policies lead to wrong policies going uncorrected and this creates other kinds of socio-economic and cultural complications.

On the other hand, the liberal-democratic system also suffers from various problems. Because of an extremely open competitive nature of its polity, taking consensual decisions take time allowing problems to multiply and getting complicated. A legal system wedded to a written Constitution also makes timely changes in strategies and legal support system difficult. On the other hand, the compulsions of electoral politics forces the political masters to support what they perceive to be populist in nature. The intellectual and public life in a liberal-democracy is also highly competitive and open. If there is a group, which feels that the naxalites should be crushed with a heavy hand, there will be other groups, which would openly denounce the strategy as undemocratic. They would say that naxalites have as much freedom to fight for their political views as those who do not agree with them have freedom to hold on to theirs. All this makes decision-making very difficult. On the other hand, it does provide a big space to those who want to dismantle this ideology and system. While the liberal democratic system allows violent movements to grow for quite some time because of its incapacity to take quick decisions, history shows that finally even a liberal democratic system hits out violently with all the resources of the State at its command leading to major turmoil, strife and violence. The liberal democratic system soon realises that its existence is at stake. Obviously, in a general atmosphere of turmoil and strife, various developmental strategies have to be put on the backburner. While the whole of India is not subjected to this kind of strife it is happening in many parts of the country and one can see how it is affecting the socio-economic development in those areas. The study team, therefore, feels that the CPI(Maoist)/naxalites and the government both should realise that a prolonged situation of peace and stability is necessary for the tribals in Bastar.

Ramchandra Guha, who was a member of 'Independent Citizens Initiative' wrote a series of articles in *The Telegraph,* Calcutta (June 26, 27, 28, 29, 2006) on his visit to Bastar wrote in the last piece: "A prime reason for the spread of Maoism, in Chhatisgarh and elsewhere, has been the failure of the State to provide remote areas with facilities for health and education and the prospect for dignified employment. It is in tribal districts in particular that the Naxalites are most active and it is tribals in particular who have gained least – and lost most – from sixty years of Indian independence. In this time, they have had to cope with an administration that is always indifferent, often corrupt, and sometimes brutal. Meanwhile, economic development has been powered in good part by wood, water and minerals found on lands inhabited by tribals and for whose profitable exploitation they have often had to make way. Recent studies show a tribal is five times vulnerable as likely as the rest of us to be displaced by a large dam, mine or steel plant. How then might the Maoist insurgency be ended or at least contained? On the Maoist side, this might take the shape of a compact with bourgeois democracy. They could emulate the Communist Party of India and the Communist Party of India

(Marxist) by participating in and perhaps even winning elections. On the government side, this might take the shape of a sensitive conceived and sincerely implemented plan to make adivasis true partners in the development process: By assuring them the title on lands cultivated by them, allowing them the right to manage forests sustainably, giving them a solid stake in industrial or mining projects that come up where they live and at the cost of their homes. In truth, the one is as unlikely as the other. One cannot easily see the Maoists give up on their commitment to armed struggle. Nor, given the way the Indian state actually functions, can one see it so radically reform itself as to put the interests of a vulnerable minority — the adivasis — ahead of those with more money and political power."

While we generally agree that an intellectual who can see the truth of a situation but is unable to write a prescription for the way out. We believe that both the state and the CPI(Maoist) can be persuaded to arrive at a peaceful resolution of the problem. After all the CPI (Maoist) should understand that the world has moved away from 1917 and 1949. They should also realise that in a situation of perpetual violence, socio-economic development of tribals whose cause they are espousing cannot take place and they may be forced to face many other uprisings similar to Salva Judum if people start perceiving that it is the violence perpetuated by them that is the real cause of their slow socio-economic development. On the other hand, the State, the government and its machinery should also be persuaded to realise that even if they think that they would finally win the battle and crush the naxalites, the collateral damages caused on the hapless tribals would have major long term political implications.

After achieving peace, the government must realise that it cannot continue to go back on its earlier mode of forcing development in tribal areas, which are unacceptable to tribals. The tribal administration would have to include benign and persuasive interactions with the tribal population so that consensus is reached about the type of development the tribals want in their area. By posting good and committed officers as well as including anthropologists and sociologists who understand tribals psyche and culture into both the educational and persuasive paradigm as well as in actual formulation of policies, the development of the tribal areas can be achieved in a peaceful manner. The study team has formalised prescriptions both for the government and the naxalites for creating an atmosphere of peace and goodwill in the area so that actual development of the area and tribals can take place. The prescription obviously is not exhaustive, as the study team does not want to suggest that it epitomises all wisdom.

Prescriptions

1. First and foremost, it is for the naxalites to make an offer for a period of prolonged peace and also offer an agenda for serious negotiations with the government. It cannot hope to be taken seriously if it maintains as it did during its talks with Andhra Government that it would continue to hold on to its weapons, run its own parallel courts, etc., but the government should release all the imprisoned naxalites. No government anywhere in the world would accept such conditions. The agenda has to incorporate rationally and logically conceived pragmatic proposals.
2. The naxalites will have to make the first offer of peace, which should include a six-month moratorium on violence perpetuated by it on so-called class enemies, Salva Judum activists and government servants and police. They should also make their intentions clear that in a phased manner they would surrender their weapons and join the political mainstream. They should realise that while the 'barrel of the gun' strategy succeeded in 1917 and 1949, the world has undergone major changes in its political and socio-economic belief systems and developmental paradigms and that it is now no more possible to defeat a state through violent insurgent means.
3. The naxalites could also start holding parallel negotiations with Left parties to form a United Left Front and can enter a combative and a competitive politics in the open political space supplied by a democratic polity. The naxalites must realise that mass base cannot be created in an atmosphere of fear and compulsion. Its coming in the open political arena

would actually give the party a real understanding of its existing mass base and may even expand it.

4. The government must also realise that development cannot take place unless there is an atmosphere of peace. It must seriously consider a genuine proposal for peace offered by the naxalites in a compassionate manner. It will have to show an understanding as to why a group still holds on to the belief of attaining power through a prolonged armed struggle. It must also realise that because of its lack of understanding of tribal culture, faulty development policies and poor 'delivery systems' in areas of governance, administration and development, it left wide spaces for a counter-ideology to grow and get entrenched.
5. The government must also realise that it cannot step up the pace of development in tribal areas, especially areas that are inhabited by primitive tribals. It must realise that if the politics of development in tribal area is undertaken without understanding the 'felt' needs of the tribals then more often than not the development becomes 'Deprivative Development', 'Discriminatory Development', or 'Differential Development'. Only 'felt need' development model can lead to an acceptable and sustainable development in tribal areas.
6. In this context it would be important to emphasise the need of recruiting anthropologists and sociologists for not only evaluating the development programmes but also to act as an interface between the tribals and the policy-makers. Because the anthropologist understands the tribal culture, ethos and demands he can not only inform the policy-makers about the concerns of the tribals but can also be used by the government to educate the tribal and genially persuade the tribals to accept necessary development schemes. It is because of the anthropologist's capacity to establish a friendly relationship with the tribals that most international institutions lay emphasis on recruitment of anthropologists for execution, evaluation and other areas of development programmes. Even ISRO had appointed anthropologists for allaying the fears of tribals and villagers in various areas where it was launching its operations.

7. Before planning any development interventions, it is important that the suspicion of the tribals is allayed. The tribal has real or presumed grievances against the more advanced cultures, which it has been carrying for ages. He has to be convinced that the members belonging to the advanced cultures and their institutions have concern and respect for them their culture, their ethos and their institutions. Before any tribal development programme can be possibly implemented certain peripheral but important actions must be taken to remove their suspicion. Attempts should be made to encourage their plays, games and sports and needs etc., can be organised on all India level. Similarly, as the tribal education has generally been non-formal in its dimensions, this will have to be synergised with the formal brand of education in a graded and gradual manner. Such small peripheral measures would break the ice and create an atmosphere where tribal-government interface can take place without much problem.
8. Development would have to be prioritised. For the tribal need of nutritious food is more important than road and electricity. Because of small land holdings, irrigation facilities become more important than credit facilities. Even today, while the tribal understands the use of money, he does not understand the complexities of a fiscal and monetary logic, which is involved in a bank credit. Similarly, need of modern medical facilities including that of nutrition supplements cannot be underestimated in tribal areas. Similarly, the importance of good and clean potable water cannot be underestimated. Most of the diseases, which afflict the tribals of Bastar can be traced to their drinking contaminated water. It must be realised that the tribal has experienced the benefits of modern medical system over the years although he still does not like belittling of his own traditional systems of witch doctors and herbal medicines.
9. The policy-maker should also understand that there is really no contradiction between economic growth of the nation with the growth and development of a geographical area inhabiting primitive tribals. One has to jettison the belief

that one has to be sacrificed for the other. If India, as a nation needs iron-ores and coal for its steel plants for its economic and industrial growth and most of the iron-ores and coal mines are situated in tribal areas, one has to find ways and means to exploit these minerals without reducing the tribal to a state of penury by dispossessing him of his land and offering him compensations which are inadequate in the long run. The way out should be creating a permanent stake of the tribal in the mining and industrial projects. One of the suggested ways is to make the tribal a shareholder in the mining or industrial projects apart from the one-time have to be formulated for general growth of the area which should also include alternative employment mechanisms, such as sericulture, cloth manufacture through hand or powerlooms, manufacture of handicrafts and artifacts, horticulture, etc.

10. It has been highlighted earlier that the tribal is a very proud and possessive about his tribal laws and customs. As in North-East, the government should think of introducing separate laws for the tribals of Bastar having consonance with their own tribal laws. Under Atricle 13 of the Constitution, 'law' includes customs or usages having the force of law. In the North-East, Garo Hills Autonomous District (Social customs and usages) Validating Act 1958, subject to any law enforced within the Garo Hills Autonomous District, all customs usages and customary practices, universally prevalent among the Garo people will have the force of law from the date the Constitution of India came into force provided that such practices, usages or customs are not against morality or public good. Something similar should be enacted for the tribals of Bastar. Similarly, when Nagaland was created a special provision relating to Nagaland was inserted in the Constitution of India by 13th Amendment Act 1962 and Naga customary law was accepted.
11. It is also important that a consultative body of traditional tribal chiefs, anthropologists and policy-makers is constituted at the district levels in the erstwhile district of Bastar (which has now been divided in 2-3 revenue districts) for deciding on the felt needs of tribals as also as a body to educate,

persuade and convince the tribals of a policy the introduction of which is felt necessary but is being resisted by the tribals. Obviously as stated above, the aforementioned prescriptions are not exhaustive and only suggestive. What is more important at this juncture is for the naxalites to realise that the likelihood of their strategy of a violent armed struggle succeeding against the might of a modern state is bleak. It would only lead to greater reprisals and counter violence. Even if we stretch our imagination to an absurd limit and agree that the possibility exists that naxalites may finally manage capture power through armed struggle, the violence, the killings and destruction for a prolonged and protracted period may leave only a debris the naxalites may find difficult to reconstruct to create a Maoist world. On the other hand, the government must also realise that in a prolonged violent war with large areas affected, violence and counter-violence would not give breathing space to the government to develop the areas which is absolutely necessary if the states and the country have to attain the levels of development they have envisaged.

Peace Initiative by Social Scientists and Independent

To
The General Secretary,
CPI (Maoist)
Sir,

Citizens: An Appeal to Maoists

We, the members of Peace Initiative Team of Social Scientists and Independent Citizens, visited Bastar area and moved around 1100 sq. kms, talked and interacted with tribals, Salva Judum supporters and CPI(Maoist) supporters in villages and *haats* to find out the reasons, dimensions and levels of violence in the area as well as to find out the possibility of peace for a creative and imaginative socio-cultural and economic development of the tribals. We came to the conclusion that unless there is a prolonged period of peace, the hapless tribals of Bastar would not only continue to suffer but no development of the tribals or the area is possible. We, however, fail to understand why the CPI (Maoist) are not able to understand this and are continuing with their romantic belief and vision of capturing state power through a prolonged and protracted violent armed struggle. We are also not able to understand why the Maoists are not able to understand the basic scientific underpinning of Marx which made him question everything in a scientific manner and come to rational conclusions. Marx, more than anyone else, realised that history never remains frozen in time and that the dialectics of cause and effect may unleash forces, which make the dialectics extremely complex, and seeing it as a simple binary conflict between thesis and anti-thesis would lead to romantic simplicity.

If this would not have been so, Leninism and Maoism would not have come into existence as both were trying to respond to the unique complex dialectics which existed in Russia of 1917 and China of 1940s. In fact, Mao even after 1949 kept on evolving new strategies which were some time successful and some time unsuccessful to response to the complex dialectic processes which undergoes sometimes complex sometimes subtle changes. Sometimes the dialectic challenges may even go unnoticed. Further the responses to these dialectic challenges have to find roots in the civilisational, cultural and ethical ecology of the area where they exist. India has certain unique civilisational, cultural and ethical psychological make-up, which abhors violence on a large scale. Any strategy whether political or social which does not accept this fact would, on long run, create problems for itself.

We, as anthropologists and social-scientists fail to understand how CPI (Maoist) leaders are not able to see this. Gandhi succeeded in his movement because he could understand this unique Indian psyche. Another fact which came to our notice during our interaction with people of Bastar area is the doubt which is now gradually growing in their minds because of contradiction between what the CPI(Maoist) leaders say and what they actually do. We would also like your response on doubts expressed by them (which are also some of our major doubts):

1. You claim to espouse the cause of the tribals and blame the state for exploiting the tribals but for the last 26 years of your stay in Dandakaranya area of Bastar, you have done very little for the development of tribals.

2. You blame the state for exploiting the tribals but you dissuade them from plucking Tendu leaf till the government agrees to a particular rate dictated by you but at the same time, you allow plucking once the corrupt contractors or their agents pay you, your share. Where does that leave the helpless tribals? Don't you see that it is because of this contradiction in your behaviour that the tribals revolted against you and the phenomena is now being called Salva Judum. Don't you see that if you give such an opportunity, any adversary would support such a movement? You thought that you would suppress the movement through brutal and violent methods but even after one and half years and death of 300-400 innocent tribals, the movement against you still continues. You have lived in Dandakaranya area for a long time to realise that the tribals of Bastar cannot be forced into a sponsored movement unless they have been greatly offended by you.
3. You claim that it is your avowed intention to clean the corrupt bureaucracy (which you term as class enemies) but you have no hesitation from collecting 'levies' and taxes from the very same corrupt officials. The tribals are also not very clear what you do with that money because he knows that very little of it is spent on his development.
4. You claim you do not harbour any anger towards ordinary and lowly paid constables, head constables and sub-inspectors as well as ordinary civilians but nobody is able to understand how you can then indulge in indiscriminate acts of killing of innocent civilians as well as lowly paid policemen.
5. You conduct your own Jan Adalats claiming that you do not have faith in the corrupt judiciary system of the country. It is then very difficult to understand why you take recourse to the same legal judicial systems and its laws to get your cadres released on bail or make efforts that your leaders in jails are treated as political criminals. Is it not better to have the honesty of a Gandhi or a Tilak or a Bhagat Singh and tell the court that you do not accept it or its laws? Your behaviour in criticising the judicial system but using it to gain benefits of freedom is interpreted as hypocrisy by even simple tribals.

6. We also came to know in our interaction with tribals of Bastar that while you do not believe in the democratic system, hoist black flags on Republic and Independence Days and call the mainstream politicians including those belonging to Left parties as corrupt and class enemies, you do have back channel contacts with the same politicians to further your personal agendas.

The aforementioned contradictions in your behaviour are not only confusing to us but have also been noticed by the tribals who claim to be your supporters and are fast leading to a sense of disenchantment. We would make an appeal to you for deep introspections. We are sure if you do so (and we are also convinced that your Party has senior leaders who can understand history, politics, theory and applications in a dispassionate manner) you would come to the conclusion that prolonged and protracted violent armed struggle would only leave destruction, debris and pain and that you can succeed in achieving your goals through a Constitutional and democratic mechanism. The peace will have to be given a chance. We think that the CPI (Maoist) leaders would have to take the initiative:

7. First and foremost it is for you to make an offer for a period of prolonged peace and also offer an agenda for serious negotiations with the government. You will not be taken seriously if you again demand as you did during your talks with Andhra Government that you would continue to hold on to your weapons, run your own parallel courts, etc. but the government should release all the imprisoned cadres. No government anywhere in the world would accept such conditions. The agenda has to incorporate a rationally and logically conceived pragmatic proposals.
8. You will have to make the first offer of peace, which should include a six-month moratorium on violence perpetuated by you on so-called class enemies, Salva Judum activists and government servants and police. You should also make your intentions clear that in a phased manner you would surrender your weapons and join the political mainstream. You should realise that while the 'barrel of the gun' strategy succeeded in 1917 and 1949, the world has undergone major changes in its political and socio-economic belief systems and developmental paradigms and that it is now

no more possible to defeat a state through violent insurgent means.

9. You could also start holding parallel negotiations with Left parties to form a United Left Front and can enter combative and a competitive politics in the open political space supplied by a democratic polity. You must realise that mass base cannot be created in an atmosphere of fear and compulsion. By coming in the open political arena you would actually get a real understanding of your existing mass base and may even expand it.

Thanking you,
With Regards, Love and Hope,
Yours Sincerely,

1. Prof S. Narayan (Anthropologist and Sociologist, Patna, Bihar)
2. Dr Ajay Kumar Singh (Patna, Bihar)
3. Mr Dhirendra Singh (Patna, Bihar)
4. Prof Mitashree Mitra (Raipur, Chhatisgarh)
5. Prof O.P. Verma (Raipur, Chhatisgarh)
6. Prof Dinesh Kumar Verma (Jagdalpur, Bastar, Chhatisgarh)
7. Dr Rajendra Singh (Jagdalpur, Bastar, Chhatisgarh)
8. Mrs Shoba Narayan (Patna, Bihar)
9. Mr Ajay Sharma (ANI/Media, Jagdalpur, Bastar, Chhatisgarh)

Peace Initiative by Social Scientists and Independent Citizens: An Appeal for Peaceful Resolution of Violence in Bastar for the Development of the Tribals and the Area

To

1. The President of India, New Delhi.
2. The Prime Minister of India, New Delhi.
3. The Union Minister of Tribal Welfare, New Delhi
4. The Governor of Chhatisgarh, Raipur
5. The Chief Minister, Chhatisgarh, Raipur.

Sir,

We, the members of the Peace Initiative Team of Social Scientists and Independent Citizens visited Bastar area and moved around 1100 sq.kms talking and interacting with tribals,

Salwa Judum supporters and CPI (Maoist) supporters in villages and haats to find the reasons, dimension and levels of violence in the area as well as to find out the possibility of peace for a creative and imaginative socio-cultural and economic development of the tribals and the area. We have come to the conclusion that a prolonged period of peace is absolutely necessary for the development of the tribals of Bastar as well as the entire area affected by violence. As social scientists we are aware that no government, especially one which adheres to a constitutional democratic polity will accept surrendering to an alternative ideology which shows open hostilities and repugnance towards a constitutional-democratic polity and structures even though it may allow to adhere to such beliefs free debating space. We are, therefore, making an appeal to CPI (Maoist) leaders to give peace a chance.

However, after stating the above, we must point out that the alternative ideologies of CPI(Maoist) could grow, capture the imagination of many as well as got entrenched due to Government's own inept handling of various development problems in tribal areas. Some of the steps, which the government will have to take once the peace if realised, are suggested as under:

(a) The government must realise that it cannot step up the pace of development in tribal areas, especially areas that are inhabited by primitive tribals. It must realise that if the politics of development in tribal area is undertaken without understanding the 'felt' needs of the tribals, more often than not, the development becomes 'Derivative Development', 'Discriminatory Development', or 'Differential Development'. Only 'felt need' development model can lead to an acceptable and sustainable development in tribal areas.

(b) In this context it would be important to emphasise the need of recruiting anthropologists and sociologists for not only evaluating the development programmes but also to act as an interface between the tribals and the policy makers.

(c) Before planning any development interventions, it is important that the suspicions of the tribals are allayed. The tribal has a litany of real or presumed grievances against the more advanced cultures, which it has been carrying for ages. He has to be convinced that the members belonging to the advanced cultures and their institutions have concern and respect for their culture, their ethos and their institutions. Attempts should be made to encourage their plays, games and sports, etc., can be organised on all India level. Similarly, as the tribal education has generally been non-formal in its dimensions, this will have to be synergised with the formal brand of education in a graded and gradual manner.

(d) Development would have to be prioritised. For the tribal need of nutritious food is more important than road and electricity. Because of small land holdings, irrigation facilities become more important than credit facilities. The need of modern medical facilities including that of nutrition supplements cannot be underestimated in tribal areas. Similarly, the importance of good and clean potable water cannot be underestimated. Most of the diseases, which afflict the tribals of Bastar, can be traced to their drinking contaminated water.

(e) The policy-makers should also understand that there is really no contradiction between economic growth of the nation with the growth and development of a geographical area inhabiting primitive tribals. If India as a nation needs iron-ores and coal for its steel plants for its economic and industrial growth and most of the iron-ores and coal mines are situated in tribal areas, one has to find ways and means to exploit these minerals without reducing the tribal to a state of penury by dispossessing him of his land and offering him compensations which are inadequate in the long run. The way out should be creating a permanent stake of the tribal in the mining and industrial projects. One of the suggested ways is to make the tribal a shareholder in the mining or industrial projects apart from the one-time compensation for his land. Alternatively, a programme will have to be formulated for general growth of the area.

(f) It is also important that a consultative body of traditional tribal chiefs, anthropologists and policy-makers is constituted at the district levels in the erstwhile district of Bastar (which has now been divided in 2-3 revenue districts) for deciding on the felt-needs of tribals as also as a body to educate, persuade and convince the tribals of a policy the introduction of which is felt necessary but is being resisted by the tribals. The government must also realise that development cannot take place unless there is an atmosphere of peace. It must seriously consider a genuine proposal for peace offered by the naxalites in a compassionate manner.

Thanking you and hoping that the government would initiate steps leading to an atmosphere of peace in Bastar area so that all-round development of the area without unnecessary stimulating the fears and concerns of tribals living in that area is made possible. Thanking you again with a hope that you would give serious thought to our study and suggestions.

Yours Sincerely,

1. Prof S. Narayan (Anthropologist and Sociologist, Patna, Bihar)
2. Dr Ajay Kumar Singh (Patna, Bihar)
3. Mr Dheerendra Singh (Patna, Bihar)
4. Prof Mitashree Mitra (Raipur, Chhatisgarh)
5. Prof O.P. Verma (Raipur, Chhatisgarh)
6. Prof Dinesh Kumar Verma (Jagdalpur, Bastar, Chhatisgarh)
7. Dr Rajendra Singh (Jagdalpur, Bastar, Chhatisgarh)
8. Mrs Shoba Narayan (Patna, Bihar)
9. Mr Ajay Sharma (ANI/Media, Jagdalpur, Bastar, Chhatisgarh)

Research Team Members

1. Prof S. Narayan (Anthropologist and Sociologist, Patna, Bihar)
2. Dr Ajay Kumar Singh (Patna, Bihar)
3. Mr Dheerendra Singh (Patna, Bihar)
4. Prof Mitashree Mitra (Raipur, Chhatisgarh)
5. Prof O.P. Verma (Raipur, Chhatisgarh)
6. Prof Dinesh Kumar Verma (Jagdalpur, Bastar, Chhatisgarh)
7. Dr Rajendra Singh (Jagdalpur, Bastar, Chhatisgarh)
8. Mrs Shoba Narayan (Patna, Bihar)
9. Mr Ajay Sharma (ANI/Media, Jagdalpur, Bastar, Chhatisgarh)

SECTION—B

Tana Bhagats Naxalism and Maoism

Introduction

Tana Bhagats are one of the tribes of Jharkhand. It is said that originally they belong to Oraon tribal group. Tana Bhagats have embraced the Kurukh Dharm or the (real or original) of the Kurukhs as they call to and are the followers of the movement called the Tana Bhagat movement. They are the only tribal groups who are follower of the Mohandas Karamchand Gandhi i.e., Mahatma Gandhi, Father of the Nation. 'Tana' means to draw thing or to pull. The Tana Bhagats resent the inferiority of their position and wish to improve it. They believe that only way to improve their condition is to practice Gandhi in their life and to follow Gandhian way of life as well as to obey God and to have right relationship with him. The correct ritual to ensure it is to give up all impure things and to purify oneself in order to worship God. Therefore, they banned all food and ceremonies which made them impure and condemned witchcraft, sorcery etc. As a result, Dharmas (God) would see that people are obeying his orders and would pull everything which harms human beings.

Tana Bhagats are generally found in Ranchi, Gumla, Lohardaga, Chatra, Palamu districts of Jharkhand state. Their total population, as reported by Ganga Tana Bhagat former MLA, is approximately 45,000. Their population is dwindling.

A network of spurs and hills covered with thick jungles are their principal abodes. Shut in between these hills and spurs lays their small hamlets almost inaccessible to an outsider. Such a country is specially suited to these jealously exclusive people and it has enabled them to maintain their isolation long after the reserve of other tribes has broken down.

In the traditional system a village community comprised a group of families, related as agnates and the administration was carried on by the village council. For social and political purposes a group of allied villages confederated together into groups known as Parhas or Pirs. Twelve to Thirty villages formed a Parha. Each Parha had its own Parha chief and Parha council. Representatives from the village council were members of the Parha council, to whom the chief was responsible. Each Parha had within its own territory—a well established form of Government through the lineage and the village, which enabled it to manage its own affairs independently. Each village is economically sufficient, it produce its own food, its playground and forest, its own village artisans, potters, weavers, blacksmiths and herdsmen. Each Parha provided for its own needs and there was a little trade or economic dependence between the Parhas. As time went on continued external threats not only forced the Parhas to submit to the authority of the tribal chief, but also to form a larger league with the neighbouring major tribes. Chotanagpur was politically united under a chief. One of the Parha chief was chosen as leader, and acquired the position of the Raja of Chotanagpur.

Tradition as well as the records of the Raja family of Chotanagpur give the detail of the election of the first Raja of Chotanagpur by the assembled Mundas and Oraons who unanimously elected Phani Mukut Rai, then chief of Khukra to be their tribal chief. Sarat Chandra Roy and Eliot think that this event took place five centuries later, after emperor Samudra Gupta of Magadh marched through the country in his southern expedition. At least we know Phani Mukut Rai was chosen as the tribal chief was given the title of the Maharaja of Jharkhand.

It was during 18th century agrarian trouble that their faith in the old tribal system was completely shaken. The Oraon saw that their old Gods and spirits failed to bring any relief and to protect them against their manifold troubles. There was a strong desire for delivery from oppressive Zamindars and money lenders as well as the new land laws etc. Consequently, a new religious movement of the old Bhagat pattern was started by the Oraons who called its Kurukh Dharm or the religion of the Kurukhs. The leaders of the new faith gave assurance to their followers that through worship to Dharmes, the only God. They would be able to raise their present degraded position to higher level as occupied by their fellow tribesmen who became Hindus or Christian converts and thus secured protection of missionaries which enabled them to improve their economic condition considerably. The religious movement was first started in April 1914 by a young man called Jatra Bhagat of the village Chipri Nawatoly of Bishunpur thana. Jatra Bhagat, when he started this movement was undergoing Matis (witchcraft) training. It is believed that one night while he was returning home after his lessons, Dharmes, the supreme God of Oraons appeared before him and told him to give up his Matiao (ghost finding and exoricison) and his belief in the blood thirsty sprits and other deities which called for animal sacrifices. God told him to stop all animal sacrifices and to give up animal food and liquor and to give up plough in their land which meant cruelty to cows and oxen, but failed to save the people from famine and poverty.

They lost faith in the land on which they where entirely dependent for their livelihood. He told the people that God does not want them to work as coolies and labourers under the zamindars or to men belonging to other castes and non-tribals. He proclaimed that he had been ordered by God to lead his people and to teach them to worship Dharmes and through worshipping Dharme they will achieve their desired goal. Thus Jatra Bhagat gave expression to the ideas which have long been fermenting in minds of the people and who where struggling to give shape to a definite tribal cult. This idea, however, was not new to the tribals of Jharkhand. The seed of freedom movement among tribals was germinated by Birsa Munda who is considered as founder of Tribal political cult, Jatra Bhagat and other prophets later gave a definite shape to this cult which exists till date.

Jatra Tana Bhagat spread like a fire in the jungle throughout the Oroan country. People refused to work for Zamindars and other non-tribals. Jatra Tana Bhagat was put behind the bar but this movement went on many local leaders took leadership in different parts of the tribal land.

Tana Bhagats believed that they can commune with God if they lived a life of ceremonial purity. Tana Bhagat gave up all kind of drinks, meat etc. They do not take food cooked by any one except those who belong to their own faith. They do not dance in Akharas, do not participate in Jatras. They do not wear coloured cloth or any kind of jwellery nor decorate their bodies with tattoo marks. During Ramgarh congress of the Indian National Congress party Gandhi Jee (Mohan Das Karamchand Gandhi) spent three days with Tana Bhagats. His three days with them has such a deep impact that even today they are following the Gandhian way of life and are practicing non-violence in true spirit. They are living the life of Gandhi. They are living Gandhi of today.

The first and the most important problem of the Tana Bhagat is land. Since they totally depend on land so it has become a burning problem for them. The Tana Bhagats whose lands were auctioned during British rule for their participation in freedom movement of the country wants to get back their land. In Bero Block only in last month their land were returned to them. During my field visit I requested each BDO/CO of Gumla, Lohardaga, Chatra, Ranchi districts to return the auctioned land of Tana Bhagats to them. They protest before the District Magistrate through nonviolence method.

It has been found during field visit that the NGO working among them for their development are exploiting them. The NGO get money for the development of Tana Bhagat which they are using in their own development. The data in hand suggest that the NGO are hand and globe for violent practices in Jharkhand.

The data in hand suggest that a special package be drafted and implemented for their development. They are the only tribal group who not only believe in Gandhian philosophy but are leading Gandhian way of life. The naxalism or the Maoism is not at all prevalent in the villages and the region in which they are living. They are ready to render their services for the development of Gandhian philosophy. They are of the opinion that if they are sent to other villages and regions where naxalism or Maoism is present they would be minimising such violent activities.

During noncooperation movement one of the freedom movements led by Mohan Das Karamchand Gandhijee Tana Bhagats stop payment of rents to their Zamindars and gave up ploughing in their field. Local police, Zamindars and money lenders reported it to the British officers. The authorities thus prohibited their gatherings and were sent to jail.

In 1921 when civil disobedience movement was started by Mahatma Gandhi throughout the country, the Tana Bhagat first joined the freedom movement, under the leadership of Sidu Bhagat of Kuru thana. Tana Bhagat believed that Jatra Bhagat was reincarnated in Gandhijee. Thus, the Tana Bhagat, movement which started as an economic and religious movement now took the shape of political movement by identifying itself with the Indian freedom movement.

In 1930 when the first no-rent campaign was started in Bardoli the Tana Bhagats were influenced by this and they stopped paying rent to the Government. There was no Congress organisation among them nor had any Congress worker informed them to do so. When they saw that Sardar Patel has started no-rent campaign at the Bardoli, they immediately stopped paying rent. The result was that their land was auctioned and today there are many landless Tana Bhagats who live as share cropper or labourers. Inspite of these they are blind follower of Gandhijee. Today, Tana Bhagats are not only Oraon but they comprise three tribes i.e., Oraon, Munda and Kharia, of these Oraon are in majority.

The Tana Bhagats are agriculturists, but the land resources of Tana Bhagats are extremely limited. The disparity in the amount of land held by individual families due to the inequalities in the number of male siblings in the family and also because of auction of their land by the Govt. for not paying rent during non-cooperation movement. Failure to restore these lands has caused widespread discontent and disappointment.

There is a growing pressure of population on the available land which makes it difficult for them to grow enough food even for subsistence.

Nontribal in tribal territory seek every opportunity to buy land from the tribesmen. The most important problem of the Tana Bhagat is that of land. Reduction of rights over Gair Mazarua land and grazing land is also causing discontent particularly among those who have no land or very little land. All such village land has now been taken over by the Revenue department. In the traditional system, such land which comprised village common was meant for public use.

Villagers fail to understand why they should not be allowed to use their own village land. Then they say, they are not allowed to clear new lands for cultivation in the forest tract because all the forest areas have been reserved by the forest department. Their another problem is the restriction put on their right to use forest products. Forest plays a very important part in the life of the tribal people. They depend very much for their subsistence on jungle produce i.e., roots, fruits, leaves, yams. These are the only food available to them during scarcity. Forests are their main source of wood for domestic purpose. The plant, roots, fruits and herbs are used as medicine or for making oil. The barks of the trees and creepers are used for making ropes. Leaves are used for making plates and rain caps, it is the grazing ground for their cattle as well the very idea that forest is denied to them gives them a great emotional shock.

Author with Block Level Officers

Tana Bhagats want to educate their children. Tana Bhagats never send their children to missionary school as they consider it against the ideology of Gandhijee. Special schools for them need to be opened.

The health of Tana Bhagat appears to be deterioriating. The main cause for ill health is poverty. There is highrate of infant mortality.

Immediately after independence the first step taken by the State Government was to pass the Ranchi District Tana Bhagat Raiyats Agricultural Land Restoration Act. This Act provided for the restoration Tana Bhagat their lands which were sold for arrears of rent between 1921 and 1942. But unfortunately even in 2011 land have not been restored to them. Some positive action is required in this direction.

Some specific programmes need to be drafted for the holistic development of Tana Bhagats.

The present study has been undertaken with specific objectives:

A Stave Engraved Names of Freedom Fighter of Tana Bhagat

Researchers with Ganga Tana Bhagat in Bero

Objectives of the Study

Tana Bhagats is such a community on which a good number of studies can be conducted. They are so fascinating that a multidimensional and multidisciplinary study could have been for academic research. But here we conducted research with focused objective; therefore we made a study on Tana Bhagat with following objectives:

1. It is proposed to have an ethnographic holistic study of the Tana Bhagat and to find out the socio-cultural ecological contents of non-presence of violence among them.
2. To find out the best impact of the Gandhian practices on neighbouring tribes.

Tana Bhagats with Author

Research Methods

Methodology: First of all the district of Jharkhand in which they live were identified. Since there is no separate census of Tana Bhagats, they are enumerated as Oraon tribe of Jharkhand even in 2011 census they are being enumerated as Oraon, so it was very difficult to identify the district. Earlier I had worked on them so I have data with me but to confirm this data I discussed it with state and district administration as well as with the Tribal Research Institute, Professors of Anthropology department, journalist, representatives of NGO etc., and finally we selected following districts of Jharkhand:

- Ranchi
- Gumla
- Lohardaga
- Palamu
- Hazaribagh
- Chatra

Then we identified one Block of each district where maximum numbers of Tana Bhagats are concentrated. Then Panchayat with maximum population of Tana Bhagat was selected. Data are collected with the help of indepth interview guide-cum-schedule. We also took help of observation method, Interview method specially focused individual and group interview, genealogical method, case study, Life history matrix etc. The collected data were tabulated and analysed. The draft report was prepared. We discussed it among ourselves and there after final report was prepared.

Field Work

Our first visit to Jharkhand for this project was in the month of November 2010. Met with the state level officers related to tribal welfare and their development as well as with the officers related to Home department of the Jharkhand Government. Then we met and discussed with District level officers and Block level officers. In this visit we collected details of the geographical distribution of the tribe. Next visit to Jharkhand was in December 2010 in which we decided the Block and the villages from where we collected research data for this study. The research instruments were finalised and researcher were recruited and properly oriented for data collection. The intensive field work, we did, from December, 2010 to April, 2011. While tabulating and analysing the field data some gaps were identified subsequently a field visit in the first half of May also took place to collect the final round of data. The first draft of report was prepared in May 2011 and then the final report was drafted for submission.

Social Life

Tana Bhagats are peace loving tribal social group. They lead very peaceful life. They maintain very harmonious and cordial relation with their neighbour.

The houses in which they live are simple. The walls are made of clay and roofs are thatched. There is one wooden door at the entrance and generally the living room and kitchen have no wooden door. Generally they do not have latrine or bathroom in their house. For cooking generally they use wood or dry leaf to cook food.

They meet with each other quite frequently. They help each other. They have a weekly meeting where they discuss their problem and its solution freely and frankly. They enjoy fair and festival together, they together try to preserve and promote Gandhian philosophy and Gandhian way of life. Their interaction is not only restricted to Tana Bhagat but their social interaction is with the neighbouring tribe whom they always persuade to follow the Gandhian philosophy and Gandhian way of life. Their social cultural interaction with the neighbours and its impact is very positive. Tana Bhagats are very simple in meeting and mixing with the neighbours and other people. Their neighbours have been seen copying their life.

Food

They are strictly vegetarian. They eat what so ever they grow. They also go to buy weekly *Haat* (Market) to purchase or sale the commodity. Generally, they eat rice. But if they grow wheat or millet or maize or any other crop then they eat that also. They resist for not purchasing any other thing except salt and match-box from market. Well or handpump are the source of water such as for drinking, cooking, washing, toilet, bathing etc. Generally they take two meals during day hours and other in the night. They do not take food cooked outside their family. Due to nonavailability of nutritious food their population is dwindling. Some affirmative programme and action is required in this regard. They grow vegetables and some fruits also but due to their poor economic condition they sell it in the market instead of consuming it. Earlier each Tana Bhagat family use to had cow and goat from whom they were getting milk but now seldom they have cow or goat. A Food policy linked with development programmes, based on their 'felt need' is required. Right to food as a fundamental right of Tana Bhagat be stored to them.

Dress

Generally they try to wear cloth produced by themselves but these day they are unable to maintain Charkha therefore they purchase Dhoti-Kurta, Gandhi topi for male and Saree and Blouse for female from Khadi Bhandar. Generally they wear white colour kurta and topi, Dhoti are obviously of white colour.

The younger generation has just started deviating dress style; some young children were observed in paint and shirt. Few youth were also observed in paint and shirt change in dress has no impact on their daily life. None of the girls were seen in non khadi dress. Tana Bhagats follow their daily life very strictly. They themselves wash their cloth. Generally they use home made detergent made from the ash of the wood, used for cooking, and a kind of clay which cleans cloth better than detergent. Their neighbouring villages are also using Khadi Dhoti and Kurta, Sari and Blouse. A policy to provide them cheaper Khadi is also required otherwise they may shift to terricotton. We ought to preserve their dress style.

Daily Life

They (including children and women) rise in early hours; go for toilet in the field, clean their teeth with twig of tree, take bath on well or hand pump, come back to courtyard of the house in which, in one corner a tricolor Gandhiflag (National flag with charkha in centre) is hoisted beside it is Tulsi plant. So they worship Gandhi flag and Tulsi and sing Bhajan which were sung by Gandhi jee. Then they take breakfast (whatsoever is available). After that they will go to their respective field and work their as per the requirement of the season. Then again in everyday life they worship Flag and Tulsi plant, whatsoever food is available in the house they eat in early evening and then spend some time discussing on issue of the family or community or read book related to Gandhi or the elderly people trained children and younger generation how to lead Gandhian way of life. They are trained from childhood to speak truth, to tolerate, never react negatively in any situation, to practice Ahimsa very strictly, not to steal anything, always eat vegetarian food, never take alcohol, even the traditional drink made in the villages are not to be taken like wise children are trained strictly in Gandhian way of life any deviation to their laid down principles of living attracts attention of the older people of the community who in turn will socialise them in their own style of life.

The socialisation process of the children of Tana Bhagats by their parents and elders of the community keep them on the path of Gandhian style of life.

The culture of tolerance and practice of nonviolence in their day to day life from very childhood under the supervision of father/mother or grandfather or grandmother helps them in leading Gandhian way of life. They never beat or scold their children even in the worst case. They just try to make the children understand, thus if they have committed a mistake and that needs to be rectified or changed without scolding him/her and telling them the correct thing to do. They always go for truth, Satyagrah, Ahimsa, Aparigraha. This is the way of their socialisation. Their neighbour gets influenced and is also practicing Gandhian way of life.

Marriage

Generally they are married at the age of 20 irrespective boy or girl. The elderly member of Tana Bhagat acts as priest. They use only five things in marriage i.e., Aksahat (rice), Haldi (Turmeric), Gur (sweet), pan (bettle leaf) and Supari (bettle nut). They lit Ghee lamp and in marriage they use earth instead of vermillion (sindur). The colour of vermillion is red and the colour of blood is also red so during freedom some of them were wounded and killed by the Britishers and their blood came out from their body hence are not using sindoor considering it as a blood of their ancestor and a symbol of Britishers.

Whenever a boy and girl is brought among Tana Bhagat through marriage then the boy or girl is properly trained to live the life with Gandhian value and philosophy. Marriages are solemnised only when they agree to adhere to live like Tana Bhagat. Marriages are performed in a simple manner. Boy and girl exchange spinned

Khadi thread which they themselves have spinned. This is the greatest gift which newly married couple exchange among themselves.

Family

The family is the basic social institution of Tana Bhagat. It is a corner stone. Fundamental value of Gandhian value and philosophy is imparted to each Tana Bhagat in his family. Three generations live together in a family i.e., grandfather, father and son. Three generations live together, share together, eat together, impart training from one generation to another generation through oral folk tradition. There is no written document of their life style or of day to day life or of their socio-cultural life. All are tradition based and are transmitted from one generation to another generation through the institution of family. They live in joint family. Head of the family is a male. Decision of the Head of the family is binding on each member. Generally decisions are taken in consultation with each member of the family. Whether the issue is small or big, each family member, child or old are involved in decision making. They never defy family decision. Each family has a Tri-Colour flag and a Tulsi plant in their courtyard.

Economy

The economy of Tana Bhagat is largely based on agriculture. They cultivate their land and grow paddy, maize, marua, Gondi etc., they eat whatsoever they grow. They purchase only matchbox and salt from the market. Majority of their land were auctioned by the British Government during freedom movement of the country. Tana Bhagat fought against the British Government on the call of Gandhi. British Government auctioned their agricultural land and forest considering that if the lands are auctioned Tana Bhagat will not fight against them but this has a reverse impact, more and more Tana Bhagat took part in the freedom movement of the country. After the independence of the country, Government of Bihar issued for restoration of all such auctioned land to Tana Bhagats which is yet to take place. Though in some Blocks lands have been returned to Tana Bhagat but it is partial return of the land in some blocks of old Ranchi districts. It has been observed that in Bero Block maximum number land has been returned to Tana Bhagat but few case of not returning of land is still continuing. In other districts i.e., Lohardaga and Gumla beginning is to be made. Therefore the issue of land and its return to each family is a primary concern for Tana Bhagat. The land is fertile and generally they go for two crops system. They use only organic fertiliser in their farm, most of Tana Bhagats have never used chemicals or pesticides in their agricultural field because they associate it with British administration. Labour for agriculture is exchanged in the community. Tana Bhagats exchange labour among themselves. They never sell their labour. Majority of them have no source of income other than agriculture.

Education

Most of the Tana Bhagats are illiterate. The reason is that the call given by Gandhijee not to study in Government schools. On the call of Gandhijee they left school and that is still continuing. They consider schooling as "Chorshiksha" (Thief education), and this belief is still continuing. However, in and around their hamlet missionary school is present in which rarely they go. Among these 'rare' we have few literate and educated persons like Ganga Tana Bhagat, Shobha Kujur etc., who has to face a lot of Ordeal. Ganga Tana Bhagat said that when he started attending school, his family did not allow him to enter kitchen and the sleeping rooms. So he was just waiting in the out house for food and was sleeping in the out house. He gave education to his daughter who passed secondary school examination.

A special school be opened among Tana Bhagats to cater their demand. The special school should impart education, in addition to regular education, the Gandhian philosophy and values. The special school should have course in basic education and also on charkha and spinning.

They should also be given technical education and vocational course. There should be special technical education for Tana Bhagats. Tana Bhagats are unable to compete with other tribes living in the region so educational institution of higher learning should have reserved seat for Tana Bhagats. Seats be reserved for Tana Bhagats, as they can't compete with other scheduled tribes, hence they need special reservation.

Tana Bhagats are not enumerated as scheduled tribe. They are not enumerated as Primitive tribe. In real situation they are more primitive than the primitive tribal groups, therefore it is suggested that Tana Bhagat needs special consideration in the field of education.

Health

The health status of Tana Bhagat also deserves special mention. They are practicing Gandhian treatment system like "Mitti Ka Lep" (clay therapy), use of herbs, roots and fruits to treat ailment related to fever, headache, anemia, waterborne diseases etc.

They seldom take allopathic medicine. They use Aurvedic medicine, therefore, it is suggested that their knowledge of herbs, roots and fruits be recorded systematically. An aurvedic public health system augmented with allopathic system also be opened in the villages of Tana Bhagats to enable them to keep them healthy. A healthy Tana Bhagat will lead healthy Gandhian life.

A training centre in basic health education and nursing be opened to train them. The preservation of their knowledge regarding health system is a must. Training centre for nurse be opened among them. Aurvedic College could be a suitable institution for preserving, promoting their health related knowledge. Their day to day practice in health system is keeping them fit for daily activity but their economy is unable to support them for healthy normal life. We have to think for multifacet approach to solve their health-related problems.

Political Life

Tana Bhagats are very simple. They do not know anything in polity other than Gandhijee. Most of them are unaware of political system and political ecology of the centre as well as of the state. But there are few like Tana Bhagat who was Member of Legislative Assembly of Bihar during 1985-1990. He was the lone MLA. In Panchayat except Shobha Kujur, none could win even as Member of Panchayat, Panchayat Samiti or Zila Parishad.

Miss Shobha Kujur won a ward member seat of Chatra Zila Parishad. Most of them feel that election has become very costly. Being follower of Mahatma Gandhi they are aware of the polity but are unable to contest due to their financial condition. Most of them are of the opinion that there should be reservation for Tana Bhagat in each seat of three tier institutions of Panchayati Raj as well as for Legislative Assembly.

Naxalism and Maoism

In course of my anthropological study on causes, nature and dimensions of violence amongst tribals in various parts of India I had occasions to visit tribal regions of Jharkhand and to interact with anthropologists, social scientists, Researchers working in the area as well as the tribals and other people living in Jharkhand. What stuck me during these interactions that Government's developmental inputs are not that high except Heavy Engineering in Ranchi, Bokaro and Jamshedpur but the naxals and Maoists response was very high in comparison to other states. Though there were some tribal tensions caused by the imposition of Forest Conservation Act but by and large, most of the tribals living in Jharkhand are happy and satisfied persons.

There is general belief held by many in Jharkhand that the violence of the nature that is now witnessed in Jharkhand was brought by the naxalites from across the border of West Bengal, Bihar, Chhatisgarh and Orissa. There is also a belief that the tribals of Jharkhand could be persuaded by the naxalites to take up arms and indulge in violence because Government has done very little for the development of Jharkhand. Even after creation of the state in 2000 could not brought development for the poor tribals. There is also a view that the tardy pace of development in the state was the result of belief that fast paced development in the area would lead to 'traumatic encounters' of the tribal with a more complex, developed and at times exploitative group of people and that the tribal of Jharkhand should be very gradually integrated into the national mainstream of thinking, economic interactions and polity.

As an anthropologist I believe that no development in Jharkhand is possible if peace does not prevail in the area. I also strongly believe that no development is possible unless the aspirations and fears of tribals of Jharkhand are taken into consideration before planning developmental strategies in the area. I further believe that the tribals of Jharkhand will not be able to freely talk about their aspirations and fears unless they get the freedom to do so. A tribal cannot freely speak his mind under threat from the Naxalites or Maoists or the Government. A situation has to be created in Jharkhand before development of the area as well as tribals living there can be earnestly undertaken. Tana Bhagats of Jharkhand is such a tribal group who are leading Gandhian way of life. They are living Gandhian. Their service may be utilised in minimising naxalism or Maoism in tribal India.

The Maoists who believe in the principle of armed struggle for bringing about a revolution and dismantling what they term as 'bourgeois capitalist democracy', have always formed a determined group amongst the Indian communists. Earlier they were part of the Communist Party of India but when the CPI started following an exclusively pro-Russian live, the pro-Maoists broke away to form the CPI(Marxist). When the CPI(Marxist) also decided to take part in Parliamentary and Assembly elections, those who considered themselves as purists broke away to form the coordinating committee of Communist Revolutionaries under the leadership of Charu Majumdar, who felt that India was ripe for an armed revolution and started his movement in Naxalbari believing in the Maoist dictum that 'a spark would cause a prairie fire'. However, when the armed struggle actually started, sharp differences arose amongst the Maoist and the movement got divided into various factions, which developed different strategies and tactics for taking the movement forward.

All the bordering districts with West Bengal were the centre for Communist revolutionaries. The forest and the hilly terrain were well known to the Maoist and it became centre of 'arm excellence'. They were freely moving to those regions. Even today most of those regions are 'freezone' for them; administration is unable to check them. But even in those region where ever Tana Bhagats are living are practicing Gandhian way of life. They do not allow Maoists to enter in their villages. On many occasions Maoists entered in the villages of Tana Bhagat who told them to cook their own food and if they start beating they never retaliate rather they told them to follow 'Ahimsa, Satya and Aparigrah'.

Maoists think that it is wastage of time to enter in their villages whenever Tana Bhagats come across with Maoists or Naxalites they preach them, request them to follow the Gandhian way of life. Maoists or Naxalites, as soon as they see a Tana Bhagat they change their way fearing that again Tana Bhagats will preach them Gandhian way of life. It is something great that Maoists or Naxalites live in and around Tana Bhagats villages but are unable to make road among Tana Bhagats. Jatru Tana Bhagats and Somari Tana Bhagats of Vishunpur of Gumla district said that at least ten maoist or naxalites changed their hearts and are living with them. This needs to be experimented in other states where Naxalism or Maoism has become a greater problem for development. We may take five or ten couple of Tana Bhagats to Chhatisgarh and Orissa and they remain their at least for three months practicing Gandhian way of life and Gandhian principle and values I firmly believe that when five or ten Maoists or Naxalites changed their heart similarly it will work in Chhatisgarh or Orissa. Only it is to be experimented under the guidance of senior anthropologists under the Supervision of Ministry of Home Affairs. I believe it is a worth experimenting in the interest of the country as well as of the tribals of India. There are few folk songs found among Tana Bhagats mentioning the importance of Satya and Ahimsa. There are few folk songs in which they are requesting Maoists or naxalites to follow the Gandhian way of life and lead a peaceful life and to bring development as suggested by Gandhi jee. These needs to be recorded, preserved and promoted local Radio Station/Television centre should record it and should telecast it. It will have tremendous impact. In the beginning one may not find much response but gradually people will get involved.

In the beginning the Naxalites or Maoists showed a fair degree of intolerance towards Tana Bhagats but gradually they started respecting them and now a few of them not only praise them but are also practicing the life style of Tana Bhagats. Tana Bhagats have shown the greatest degree of tolerance and faith in 'Satya and Ahimsa' which lured few of Naxalites and Maoists. In Tandwa of Chatra district of Jharkhand recently a good number of

Naxaliltes and Maoists are spending their life as Tana Bhagats and are willing to lead the life of Tana Bhagat in future also. We should sincerely and seriously think for it. Ranka Ram Goenda Tana Bhagat and Uragaon Thakur Tana Bhagat of Needra village of Chandwa, Latehar, Palamu is a freedom fighter and claims that some of Naxalites and Maoists got influenced by his Gandhian style of life and now they are firm believer in Gandhi's Satya and Ahimsa and are leading almost the life of a Tana Bhagat. He further said that Government should have some policy to support.

Tana Bhagats are helping Naxalites or Maoists to adopt Gandhian way of life. Whenever and who ever come and stay with them get influenced by their style of life and world view. He further said that 'Bullet' is not a solution of Naxalism or Maoism if we get chance we may influence them to adopt our life style and be follower of Satya, Ahimsa and Satyagrah. Another Tana Bhagat named Musari of Siram Bandidera, Balumath, Latehar, Palamu is of the view that if an opportunity comes he is ready to visit Naxal or Maoist effected tribal villages of Orissa and Chhatisgarh and to stay for three months to convert the tribals as well as Naxalites and Maoists in the Gandhian life style. They are ready to turn it into a social cultural movement and he is of the opinion that this will have definite impact in minimising Naxalism and Maoism if not in completely removing it. He is further of the opinion that given the opportunity for long term experiment they will definitely achieve success in restoring peace. They say that they are the follower of Mahatma Gandhi when he can bring freedom to country by Satya, Ahimsa and Satyagrah they are willing to go for removing violence like Naxalism and Maoism from the country.

Jirangi Tana Bhagat of Thathaugi, Tandwa of Chatra district feel that some tribal Naxals and Maoists be also realise that in situation of perpetual violence, socio-economic development of tribals whose cause they espousing can not take place and they may be forced to face many other uprisings if people start perceiving that it is the violence perpetuated by them that is the real cause of their negligible development. On the other hand, the state, the Government and its machinery should also be persuaded to realise that even if they think they would finally win the battle and crush the Naxalities, the collateral damages caused on the poor tribals and Tana Bhagat would have major long term political implications.

Ram Tana Bhagat of Nindra, Chandwa, Latehar, and Palamu is of the view that 'after achieving peace, the Government must realise that it cannot continue to go back on the earlier mode of forcing development in tribal areas which are unacceptable to tribals. The tribal administration would have to include benign and persuasive interactions with the tribal population so that consensus is reached about the type of development the tribals want in their area. The policy and programmes of the socio-economic development of the tribals be drafted on their 'Feltneed'. Their 'Feltneed' based programmes are neglected for last sixty three years resulting into unrest and violence of various natures in tribal India. By posting good and committed officers as well as including anthropologists who understand tribal psyche and culture into both the educational and persuasive paradigm as well as in actual formulation of policies, the development of the tribal areas can be achieved in a peaceful manner.

Data at hand suggest that Tana Bhagat can play important role in minimising the Naxalism and Maoism in tribal India. Ganga Tana Bhagat of Bero, Ranchi feels that he met with Pandit Nehru, Srimati Indira Gandhi and Rajeev Gandhi but he could not get desired response from them. A few days contact with Mahatma Gandhi changed their heart, for any problem they adopt 'Satyagrah' and their problems are looked into. They never took the violence as a tool for the solution of their problem. Therefore, Ganga feels, that they have great responsibility towards the tribals of India in bringing positive change in their social, economic, education and health conditions.

In one of my Book i.e., 'Sustainable Development' I have mentioned that the development inputs induced among tribals of India in last sixty three years has resulted into "Deprivatory Development", "Discriminatory Development" and "Differential Development". Let us be very honest to Tana Bhagats and the tribals of the tribal India and let us address the problem at the root. The causes at the root is their 'holistic exploitation', 'Developmental inputs not reaching to them in real term', 'planning for their development is not based on their 'felt need'.

Further the blaming of state Government that Government at centre has not given full support in curbing Naxalism or Maoism and similar political statement needs careful policy consideration so far Naxalism or Maoism or such other movements are concerned. The blaming game by State Government must stop in the interest of the country. It has been further observed that the infirmity in action and sharing of information is a must among paramilitary forces and state police.

In contemporary Indian scenario there is a social group practicing Satya and Ahimsa. They depend solely on what soever they produce. They cultivate rice, wheat, vegetables, papaya, mango, guava etc., on their own land. They also grow cotton to spin for making their cloth. They believe that as Gandhijee was wearing Khadi dhoti so they wear Khadi Dhoti Kurta and a Gandhi cap on their head and a Tiranga (Tri Colour Indian National Flag) in their hand. They are living Gandhi and firm believer in Satya, Ahimsa, Shanti, Aparigraha, Xshma, Sehanshilta and Dan. They may play important role in minimising or even removing Naxalism or Maoism under a long term strategy for restoring peace in the country.

Recommendations

1. Restoration of land. Their land were auctioned by the British Government, are yet to be restored to Tana Bhagat.
2. Agriculture clubbed with Horticulture and Floriculture be promoted. Medicinal plant be also promoted.
3. Irrigation facility be made available to Tana Bhagat.
4. Special school for Tana Bhagat be started.
5. Industrial Training Institute imparting training in Charkha-prepration, use and maintenance of charkha be imparted to them in addition to other vocational course.
6. Market for charkha and its product be provided to them.
7. Tana Bhagat cultures need to be preserved and promoted.
8. It is their tradition and culture which helps them in preserving and promoting Gandhian value and Gandhian way of life.
9. Youth and elderly members of Tana Bhagat may be taken to Chhatisgarh, Orissa, and Maharastra etc., and be allowed

to interact and stay atleast for a month with them. If such visit make difference then a periodical visit may be undertaken in other states as a measure to minimise Naxalism and Maoism.

10. The impact of nonviolence, Satyagrah and truth will take some time but it is worth doing experiment. If it brings even 10 per cent change in the beginning it will have wonderful impact in long term experiment in curbing Naxalism and Maoism and such other similar violence.
11. The visual presentation of the Tana Bhagat if projected through national electronic channel is bound to have positive impact. The public relation department or tribal welfare department should organise screening film on Tana Bhagat in Chhatisgarh, Orissa, Andhra Pradesh etc.
12. Demographically they are dwindling therefore health inputs on priority basis are required.
13. Policy, Plan and Programme ought to be environmental and ecological friendly as well as Tana Bhagat friendly.
14. Teachers appointed at primary level should be from Tana Bhagat community and in middle; high school level should be Tana Bhagat friendly.
15. Tana Bhagat are living Gandhi. Their life style, world view, ethos inspires others to follow them. A few cases of converting heart of Naxalites or Maoist to Tana Bhagat life have been reported; if they have interface with the tribals of Chhatisgarh, Orissa, Andhra Pradesh may have positive impact in minimising or removing Naxalism or Maoism. I strongly recommend to take them in a group of five or ten or as convenient to Bastar region of Chhatisgarh and also in Orissa, Andhra Pradesh etc., it will firmly, slowly remove Naxalism and Maoism.
16. There are several Naxals/Maoists group operating in Jharkhand but majority of them are the lumpen elements and are concerned more in extracting money from contractors, businessman etc., than for the development of the people this need to be widely publicised by those Naxalites/Maoists who are arrested by the police in order to minimise or curb Naxalism/ Maoism in the region. These

lumpen elements have international connection and generally work on their dictates.

17. Development programme must reach to the target group.
18. Political parties should not be allowed to use Maoists or Naxalites to be used as an instrument for winning elections. Election Commision should take note of it.
19. Panchayat, Panchayat Samiti and Zila Parisad be given more power and functions for the development of people. If the Naxalites or Maoists start participating in Panchayati raj institutions, it will also help in minimising or removing Naxalism or Maoism.
20. Development would have to be prioritised. For the Tana Bhagats need of nutritious food is more important than road and electricity.
21. Tana Bhagats is encouraged to take initiative in neighbouring villages to create a situation so that Naxalites or Maoists may not enter those villages as they are not entering to Tana Bhagat's villages.
22. The policy-maker should also understand that there is really no contradiction between economic growth of the nation with the growth and development of a geographical area inhabiting Tana Bhagats. One has to jettison the belief that one has to be sacrificed for the other. If India as a nation needs iron-ores and coal for its steel plants for its economic and industrial growth and most of the iron-ores and coal mines are situated in tribal areas, one has to find ways and means to exploit these minerals without reducing the tribal to a state of penury by dispossessing them of their land and offering them compensations which are inadequate in the long run. The way out should be creating a permanent stake of the tribal in the mining and industrial projects. One of the suggested ways is to make the tribal a shareholder in the mining or industrial projects apart from the one-time compensation for his land. Alternatively, a programme will have to be formulated for general growth of the area which should also include alternative employment mechanisms such as Charkha spinning, spinning of cotton, cloth manufacture through hand or powerlooms, sericulture,

floriculture, manufacture of handicrafts and artifacts, horticulture etc.

23. It is also important that a consultative body of Tana Bhagats, anthropologists and policy-makers be constituted at the district levels in the districts of Ranchi, Gumla, Lohardaga, Palamu, Latehar and Chatra for deciding on the 'felt needs' of the Tana Bhagats as also as a body to educate, persuade and convince the Tana Bhagat of a policy the introduction of which is felt necessary. Obviously, the above recommendations are not exhaustive and only suggestive, what is more important at this juncture is for Tana Bhagats to realise their use as an instrument in minimising and removing Naxalism and Maoism. At the same time the Naxalites and the Maoist should also realise that the likelihood of their strategy of a violent armed struggle succeeding against the might of a modern state is bleak. It would only lead to greater reprisals and counter violence even if we stretch our imagination to an absurd limit and agree that the possibility exists that naxalites may finally manage capture power through armed struggle, the violence, the killing and destruction for a prolonged and protracted period may leave only a debris the Naxalites may find difficult to reconstruct to create a Maoist world. On the other hand, the Government must also realise that in a prolonged violent war with large areas affected violence and counter violence would not give breathing space to the Government to develop the area which is absolutely necessary if the states and the country have to attain the levels of development they have envisaged. Here is a community known as Tana Bhagats the living Gandhians, may be used as an instrument, under designed strategy, to minimise and gradually to remove Naxalism or Maoism in the country.

Summing Up

To sum up it can be very safely concluded that the Tana Bhagats are the only living social group who are following Gandhian way of life, Gandhian values and ideals and firmly believe in practicing non-violence, Satya, Ahimsa non-cooperation, Aparigrah which placed them on very high pedestal in the world. They are the only living Gandhian of the world.

The content of their culture are tolerance of extreme degree. On several occasions Naxalites or Maoists entered their villages, asked for food, money, be carrier of their arms, ammunitions etc. Tana Bhagats refused for which Naxalites or Maoists beat them but they remain calm, cool, composed and never reacted. Their repeated behaviour impressed some of Naxalites or Maoists to adopt the life of Tana Bhagat. It suggests that in the long run, if Tana Bhagats are used as an instrument for minimising removing Naxalism or Maoism is bound to succeed. If this experiment is conducted in Chhatisgarh, Orissa, Andhra Pradesh etc., will definitely bring positive change in the incidence of Naxalism. Tana Bhagats believe that "Mohan Das Karamchand Gandhi" popularly known as Gandhijee has brought independence to the country only by experimenting these methods. Then it will also work in minimising and removing Naxalism or Maoism. Bullet for Bullet or green hunt is no solution. It has not brought any change rather it has increased from one district to several districts, from one state to several states. The administration ought to have sensitive and not only people-oriented but also people- friendly. Tana Bhagat is a rare tribal group of the world, they be recorded visually. Their visual presentation in the Naxal or Mao inflicted region will have positive impact. Their continuous broadcast or telecast will definitely change the heart of Naxalites or Maoists. Our field data suggest that we have several such examples of Naxalites or Maoists who changed their heart after meeting with Tana Bhagats.

Tana Bhagats deserve attention of the administration for their welfare and development. The policy and programmes be drafted and implemented for their welfare and development under the supervision and consultation of anthropologist deeply associated with them. Their socio-economic development may further empower them to minimise the Naxalism or Maoism effectively.

Gandhi and his ideals, way of life and practices is the only solution of violence in global perspective. The holistic approach of the Tana Bhagat's life style and practice of Ahimsa, Satya, Aparigrah, Xchama, devotion to one's work etc., are the solution of violence in tribal India such as Naxalism, Maoism etc., world has witnessed Gandhi and his philosophy, style of life, the only solution to violence. Naxalism or Maoism is also violence. Here we have a tribe Tana Bhagat, living Gandhi, let us project them to be used as an instrument for bringing peace.

Research Team

1.	Professor S. Narayan	Patna
2.	Mrs Shobha Narayan	Patna
3.	Dr Prabhat K Singh	Ranchi
4.	Sri Jagdeep Oraon	Ranchi
5.	Sri Rajesh Roshan	Ranchi
6.	Ms Shobha Tana Bhagat	Ranchi
7.	Mr Jaipal Tana Bhagat	Ranchi
	Computer and Software Experts	
8.	Vishwajit Kumar	Patna
9.	Tabassum Naz	Patna

Summary

Naxalism and Maoism is a social and economic problem but more so it is now a problem of internal security. The experts of internal security feels that the problem of Naxalism and Maoism is growing because of political patronage. In early 70s counted blocks and villages were the centre of Naxalism and Maoist movement but in current scenario almost each state of the country is suffering from this problem. This is being consiered as the problem of law and order and also of administration but social scientist hold different opinion. They feel that the problem of Naxalism and Maoism is because of the failure of the policy and plan meant for the development of people of the country.

In foregoing pages it has been made clear with field data that the development policy and programmes could not percolate to the ground reality resulting into high level of corruption in the system and it further led to dissatisfaction among masses which culminated into a movement called Naxalism and Maoist movement. The so-called naxal and maoist cader took advantage of dissatisfaction of the people and started attracting them to their own group to solve their problem in the village itself.

Working in tribal/rural/urban India for more than 60 years I am of the opinion that this problem can be solved very easily by creating rapport with the people. The system is considerd alien by the people. The 'felt need' deserve urgent consideration by the policy and programme-makers. Those who are involved in the and programme for the development must be a man of integrity and honesty. The monitoring of the programme also required senior and serious people. I have dealt with two very simple examples in the foregoing pages i.e., Mineral Development corporation located in the interiors of Dantewada has failed to implement the rehabilitation programme of the displaced population whose land were acquired almost 65 years back has not been settled and rehabilitated till date forcing them to go to the fold of Naxalism and Maoism. I also noticed the same case in Sipat where NTPC acquired land for their project but failed to implement the rehabilitation and resettlement policy and programme for those whose land were acquired.

In road construction from Jagdalpur, Dantewada to Hyderabad, DRDO were facing uphill task in constructing the road, a good number of DRDO personnel were killed by the Naxal and Maoist group. A group of social scientist's suggested to the ministry that please make a road a little zig-zag to avoid demolish the workship place and burial place of the local population. Further, it was also suggested that the local population must be involved in the construction of road. These advices were followed and today road is their and all kind of traffic is their.

I am sure that if we are sincere to solve the problem with honesty in the interest of the people of India then this problem can be solved and if we are playing poilitics in the name of problem then it will only linger and the solution is far far away.

Index

C

N

R